T0335339

GREAT

DISCOVER THE GREAT PLAINS

Series Editor: Richard Edwards, Center for Great Plains Studies

PETER J. LONGO

PLAINS

Politics

UNIVERSITY OF NEBRASKA PRESS   *Lincoln and London*

A Project of the Center for Great Plains Studies, University of Nebraska

Library of Congress
Cataloging-in-Publication Data
Library of Congress Cataloging-
in-Publication Data
Names: Longo, Peter Joseph, author.
Title: Great Plains politics / Peter J. Longo.
Description: Lincoln: University of Nebraska
Press, 2018. | Series: Discover the Great Plains
| "A Project of the Center for Great Plains
Studies, University of Nebraska." | Includes
bibliographical references and index.
Identifiers: LCCN 2017056786
ISBN 9780803290716 (pbk.: alk. paper)
ISBN 9781496210630 (epub)
ISBN 9781496210647 (mobi)
ISBN 9781496210654 (pdf)
Subjects: LCSH: Great Plains—Politics
and government—Citizen participation.
| Community life—Great Plains—
History. | Great Plains—Biography.
Classification: LCC F591 .L636 2018 |
DDC 978—dc23 LC record available at
https://lccn.loc.gov/2017056786

Set in Garamond Premier by E. Cuddy.

This work is dedicated to Rick Edwards and
in memory of Amy and Charlie Longo

CONTENTS

ILLUSTRATIONS

ACKNOWLEDGMENTS

This project first and foremost acknowledges Richard Edwards, the director of the Center for Great Plains Studies at the University of Nebraska–Lincoln. Rick Edwards guided and encouraged me throughout the project. He was patient and kind enough to read numerous drafts throughout various stages of this work. His insightful comments allowed me to complete this project.

Thanks to Joyce Holland, great-granddaughter of Junius Groves. Joyce and I had several conversations and email exchanges regarding her grandfather. I thank Joyce and her extended family, especially Mary Kimbrough, Groves's great-grandniece, who provided me with several insights as well. Thanks to Claude Louishomme who made a visit to Joyce Holland on my behalf.

Thanks to Tom Tye for sharing his thoughts and insights on Virginia Smith.

I was fortunate to have several student assistants throughout the project. Thanks to Andy Huynh, Taylor Reichardt, Carly Brown, and Tanner Stark. Jessa Schultis was so very helpful and patient throughout the entire project. Amanda Slater provided a careful read with comments, as did Dennis Seberger. Thank you to all of my students. I also thank Peterson (Pete) Brink, an archivist at the University of Nebraska–Lincoln. And thanks as well to my helpful office staff—Mary Kay Blanchard, Barb Wayman, and Peg Holen.

Molly Spain provided helpful suggestions and edits. Melissa Amateis provided essential assistance and edits that accelerated the completion of the project.

Kate Schneider offered her splendid photographs. The Center for Great Plains Studies provided generous research support, my colleagues at the center offered thoughtful conversation, and the administration at the University of Nebraska at Kearney (especially Vice Chancellor Charles Bicak) provided me with a semester research leave. My colleagues in the Political Science Department offered encouragement and support throughout the project. Thanks to Katie Nieland of the Center for Great Plains Studies for her cover art and to Nathan Putens for the cover and book design.

Thanks to my colleagues John Falconer and Chuck Rowling for reading and commenting on an early draft.

Special thanks to Professor John Hibbing of the University of Nebraska–Lincoln, Professor Joan Blauwkamp of the University of Nebraska at Kearney, and Professor James Scott of Texas Christian University for their careful review and comments on the draft. They provided me with the insights to move to the finish line. And thanks to Joe Blankenau of Wayne State College for his comments.

I wish to thank the professional editorial staff at the University of Nebraska Press. Alisa Plant, Courtney Ochsner, Joeth Zucco, and Anna Weir and all who were so very helpful during the completion of this project.

There were so many friends and colleagues as well as my wife, children, grandchildren, and siblings who shored me up throughout this project. I am forever grateful. In the end, I assume all responsibility for errors in the manuscript.

The title of this book may require some explanation. Political scientists both past and present have been concerned with governing and how good politics can lead to good governing. Media pundits often overemphasize elections, with chatter mainly focusing on data to predict or explain electoral outcomes. But it is not terribly exciting or meaningful to boldly predict that Kansas—or fill in the name of any Great Plains state you wish—will elect a Republican. Given the current contentious conversations but repeating outcomes, many people have lost interest in politics defined in this way. What may be of more interest are the multiple and sometimes surprising ways in which people go about organizing daily life in their own communities. My title, *Great Plains Politics*, is intended to suggest this subtler political identity of the Great Plains—an identity measured not by mounds of voting data but in the community actions of its people. From the outset I want to suggest that the concept of *politics* extends beyond formal office holding. Politics in the Great Plains is inextricably linked to community.

Understanding politics and place has long occupied scholars and other interested observers, and it plays a particularly outsized role in the Great Plains. Aristotle, one of the first political scientists, addressed, among other topics, politics and place. To be a good citizen, he argued, requires participation in the deliberative nature of the community, and as we will see, citizens of the Great Plains routinely engage in just this way. Political activity best defines the Great Plains. Space, or place, becomes the foundation of regional identities. An acquired sense of place serves to help one know oneself, promotes a sense of community, and builds insight into the human condition and

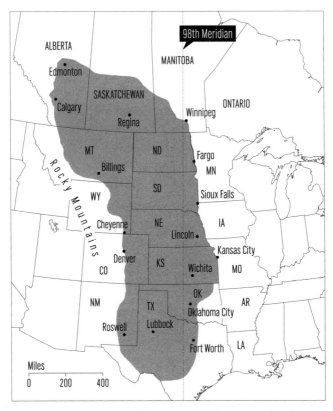

1. The Great Plains. Created by Katie Nieland, 2017. Used with permission.

the natural ecology of place. We will see time and time again that people in the Great Plains build their identities through their actions as participants with the collective citizenry.

To illustrate the importance of this collective citizenry, I will focus on six remarkable people: Wilma Mankiller, a citizen advocate and the first woman to serve as chief of the Cherokees; Virginia Smith, a Republican U.S. representative from Nebraska's rural and expansive Third Congressional District; Junius Groves, a former slave who walked from Kentucky to Kansas, where he built a thriving farm and contributed to the greater Kansas community; George McGovern, a U.S. representative and senator from South Dakota, Democratic presidential candidate, and "food ambassador"; Robert Dole, a Kansas congressman and senator who also was a (Republican) presidential candidate and a "food ambassador"; and Harriet Elizabeth Byrd, the first African American elected to serve as a Wyoming state representative. These six leaders will illustrate that the politics of the Great Plains builds on a common and deep commitment to community, and the individuals featured here were extraordinary Great Plains community builders. Before exploring their stories, I provide a snapshot of the Great Plains to sketch the context in which they worked.

The Great Plains is a vast, semiarid, thinly populated region. It is one of the great grasslands of the world, with a well-known variation in weather but a perhaps surprising variation in topography, in land cover and wildlife, and in the people and cultures of those who inhabit it. Perhaps because it is mostly treeless and without mountains and oceans, outsiders from more humid places often fail to appreciate its beauty or its bounty. It has often been dismissed as being of little worth, receiving harsh treatment from national commentators who suggest there may be little of value here to merit study or understanding. In 1823 Stephen Long, leading a government expedition to explore it, published a map that branded the region as "the Great American Desert," at the time not considered an appealing appellation. In 2002 the *New York Times* columnist Nicholas Kristof wrote, "It's time for us to acknowledge one of America's greatest mistakes, a 140-year-old scheme that has failed at a cost of trillions of dollars, countless lives and immeasurable heartbreak: the settlement of the Great Plains."

Yet others—academics, residents, and travelers through the area—with perhaps more intimate familiarity with the region's charms, have found much to interest them, including the resilient, civic-minded culture constructed by the residents of the region. This culture not only sustains a vital population but gives the region its distinctive character. Modest Great Plains residents and their subtle surroundings are not attention grabbing. What Kristof's dismissive portrait most suggests is the need for books like this.

In a thinly settled region, population growth or loss becomes a closely watched and much-worried-about issue. The Great Plains, like other regions where farming is a principal occupation, has experienced rural population decline resulting from farm consolidation and the persistent improvement of productivity-enhancing machinery. Yet the overall population of the region is relatively stable, so what has occurred is a shifting of the population from country to town, from very small places where high schoolers play six-man football to bigger ones where they send out eight-man squads, and from smaller towns to cities. Metropolitan areas and smaller cities across the Great Plains have grown—for example, Grand Island (Nebraska) had a population of 43,613 in 2000, but by 2015 it had grown to 51,440; Rapid City (South Dakota) grew from 52,980 residents in 2000 to 73,569 in 2015; and Wichita (Kansas) increased from 344,284 in 2000 to 389,624 in 2015. As larger communities grew, other rural towns, especially very small ones, declined. Both situations—growing populations and declining ones—place a premium on community building. Declining population, by putting the very existence of the community at risk, especially requires deeper commitments from the remaining residents. They may engage in the occasional hand-wringing, but many residents of small communities know how to persevere and accentuate the value of community life.

Social capital can be defined as the bonds and shared values that connect individuals and on which they rely to make a community work. Famed political scientist Robert Putnam has underscored the importance of social capital for residents' well-being in any community. But in the Great Plains, associational virtues are especially critical to the persistence and quality of community life, and in the region's successful communities, such bonds are abundant and strong. For example, Richard Edwards used the town of Stanley, North Dakota, before its oil boom to illustrate the virtues that Stanley residents admired and aspired to. He observed, among others, the virtues of resoluteness, "a kind of implacable acceptance and embracing of what needs to be done regardless of inconvenience or possible danger"; of steadfastness, "being a reliable person whom others could count on every day"; and of devotion to community, "[pitching] in to improve the community's life without expecting anything in return." The story of Old Stanley provides insight into the "fragile values" that lead to viable community life. The importance of civic or community values has been demonstrated time and time again by residents throughout Great Plains history.

Great Plains communities, much as they are built on social capital, are like others in that they also have negative elements running through them. Great Plains history carries its full share of racism, sexism, antisemitism, anti-Catholicism, nativism, and homophobia. Some of the region's political leaders even embraced these negative ideas; one was Nebraska's J. Sterling Morton (founder of Arbor Day and a nineteenth-century U.S. secretary of agriculture), who fought to keep African Americans from constitutional standing in his state. The Ku Klux Klan (KKK) was for a time active in both small and large communities in the region. Sadly, discrimination, hate, bullying, segregation, gossip, and other rejections thus also form part of the region's political layout, current and past.

Corrupt actions harm not only the human spirit but the region's fragile ecology as well. During the great North Dakota oil boom of the early 2000s workers flooded into small traditional communities, overwhelming those communities' social capital and introducing new and destructive elements. The exploitation of natural resources in North Dakota and other Great Plains states and provinces often proved detrimental to the long-standing character of surrounding communities. The lure of money, while bolstering census numbers and corporate bank accounts, often undercut the political bonds needed to support communities. Throughout the Great Plains, as in Old Stanley, social capital is built on the values and virtues prized by communities, which lead to positive political activity. Indeed, we will find social capital in the form of positive political associations working in all the communities we explore. Virtuous living is an ambitious but important aim, even when missed from time to time. Negative components of life on the Great Plains were and are real, but the components most unappreciated are the positive virtues of politics that sustain community life.

This book will unearth the shared values that result in a vibrant life on the Great Plains. The willingness of residents to be actively engaged in the lives of others fuels their political drive. We will explore how community leaders, especially the six we feature, readily shared their talents with others in order to perpetuate strong community life. Community successes can be as varied as the climate found in the Great Plains, and they suggest that the sustainability of the region is a result of positive civic behavior rooted in the realpolitik of the people. Political contributions sustain life, and while rural population decline in the Great Plains is an empirical reality, the region's civic character is worth exploring as a key element in the resiliency of Great Plains communities.

GREAT PLAINS POLITICS

CHAPTER 1

Wilma Mankiller

Grassroots Activism to Leading the Cherokee Nation

Tahlequah, Oklahoma, the home of Wilma Mankiller, is on the eastern Oklahoma cusp of the Great Plains, which gives rise to the Ozark Uplift. From the uplift, if one strains one can see the rolling Great Plains. Mankiller was born in 1945, several generations removed from the physical Trail of Tears but metaphysically always a part of the path. Her political life reveals many attributes that derive from her Cherokee roots. Place is often defined by its physical space but can also refer to the social connections among people living within a particular location. Knowledge and appreciation of one's place is vital for understanding community life and for perspective on how one might serve the greater community. Cherokee heritage defined Mankiller's sense of place.

Mankiller's upbringing was shaped by family, fellow Cherokees, and broader Native traditions. The Cherokees settled in Oklahoma under much different terms than white settlers, who were for the most part voluntarily lured to the state by promises of cheap land and fulfilling notions of manifest destiny. As forced settlers, the Cherokees turned their collective attention to making the best of a malevolent government decision. Bad politics and hurtful policies provided the Cherokees with their Oklahoma home. Good politics, from the likes of Mankiller, would create opportunities there for the tribal community.

2. Wilma Mankiller, first woman chief of the Cherokee Nation. Wilma Mankiller Foundation.

Mankiller for a time was the leader of her fellow Cherokees and of community members in Tahlequah. For her many accomplishments, she was a serious candidate to replace Andrew Jackson as the face on the twenty-dollar bill. (Harriet Tubman, another major contributor to community life, was chosen instead.)

The Cherokees' sense of place is muddled due to forced settlement. While they have always possessed an appreciation of their culture, their connection to their physical place was disrupted when Presidents Andrew Jackson and Martin Van Buren forced them to leave their ancestral lands, relocating them from the Southeast to Oklahoma. The Indian Relocation Act, urged by Jackson, set in motion treaty negotiations and removal in 1838 under Van Buren. The Nun-da-ut-sun'y (trail where they cried), most commonly known as the Trail of Tears, was a daunting reality, as roughly four thousand of the seventeen thousand Cherokees died in the forced move. Despite their forced relocation, the Cherokees eventually forged a sense of place in Oklahoma.

Oklahoma became a state in 1907. Legal constructs defined the Oklahoma boundaries, but the coexistence of the Cherokee Nation and Oklahoma remains a story still in progress. Cherokee culture shaped community life early on, and many aspects of the state resulted from its multiracial development. Of the three hundred thousand Cherokees, more than one hundred thousand live within the boundaries of Oklahoma. The multicultural relations between Cherokees and other settlers is part of the essence of Oklahoma.

Mankiller's earliest understandings of politics and community life were derived from her Cherokee foundation and the facets of place surrounding her. The Cherokee philosophy was the major catalyst for her political work. Cherokees draw strength from each other and not from material accumulations. Mankiller's politics were shaped by an understanding of community good, not just individual wealth. An examination of Mankiller's heritage and experiences will lead to a better understanding of the political contributions she made to her community, the state of Oklahoma, and beyond.

Early Years: Developing a Sense of Place

Economic austerity was very real to Mankiller. Her family was poor, and the influences provided by material wealth were absent. In her 1993 autobiography, she writes, "We were not well off, at least when it came to money. Like many of the people in Adair County, we were really poor—'dirt poor'—is how they say it in Oklahoma." But there was a richness to her life. As she explains, "There were always lots of children to run and play with, and laughter and no set bedtime." She grew up surrounded by a loving family and friends and the gifts of the natural world. Tahlequah was her home, her community, her place of security. It is not likely that a preteen Mankiller was contemplating her role as a political leader. Her politics were guided by her family, and her sense of security was reinforced by family and the familiar surroundings of her place. The place just happened to be in Oklahoma. But as time passed, her identity became grounded in that place. The understanding of place has many layers—land, people, family, tradition—and this understanding would guide Mankiller's journey as she traveled through life.

Mankiller's path from childhood to adulthood was difficult. At the age of eleven, in 1956, the comfort of living in Tahlequah ended when her father decided to uproot the family and move to California. The move was generated by yet another ill-conceived federal program, one that aimed to "urbanize" Native Americans.

As Mankiller was uprooted from her childhood place of comfort, she lost a loving community and physical atmosphere that had surrounded her for years. Despite repetitive pleas, as an eleven-year-old she did not have the political clout in her family to sway decision-making, so off she went with her family. California had little appeal to the young Mankiller. Despite her young age, she had already developed a keen sense of place. California would offer her many enduring lessons, but at the time, the move made no sense to her. Adolescents, Mankiller included, typically do not conjure up ways in which a move can somehow provide leadership development; the goal for most is to stay in control of their personal identity. By most accounts, she would have rather stayed in Oklahoma.

In a metaphysical sense, she likely never left her Cherokee home. In a *New York Times* article, reporter Sam Howe Verhovek said that Mankiller remarked, "I remember as we drove to the train, I felt so sad. I wasn't excited at all. I was trying to memorize every tree, and what the school looked like, which flowers were blooming in my grandfather's front yard, all those sorts of things."

She would remember the land. The trees would give way to the Oklahoma plains as she traveled through the state and onward to California, a place that never quite captured her attention and certainly did not define her essence. The family was relocated to the Bay Area, but the Bay Area was not to be the final destination for Mankiller. Her interest, even as she matured into womanhood, was instilled in Oklahoma. California, although a land of opportunity for many, was the destination of her own Trail of Tears. But she lived in the Bay Area through her midtwenties, and as a result, California and the political events of the sixties and seventies enriched her political knowledge and understanding. Like so many Cherokees, Mankiller made the best of the move. Still, her gaze and love of her childhood place on the cusp of the plains did not wane. The lessons she gathered from

California were many, and they only complemented her Tahlequah groundings.

California politics also provided opportunities and experiences that added to Mankiller's overall worldview. She volunteered in Native American centers, joined the occupation of Alcatraz, and engaged in a variety of other political activities in the state. Political activism can be acquired in diverse settings, and likewise, it does not know boundaries. Mankiller made the most of her time in California to learn how to contribute to the greater community life. Still, she keenly remembered her childhood in Oklahoma, and her deep affection for it brought her back home. She had learned to serve with and for others; in this regard, she embodied *gadugi*—the characteristic of working together. Now she would apply those lessons where they counted most.

Returning Home: Political Activism in Oklahoma

In the late 1970s Mankiller and her two daughters returned to Oklahoma. From her family perch, she would dream and plan how she might best serve her Cherokee people. Her dreams were delayed, however, when she was involved in a near-fatal automobile accident. She recovered slowly, and the recovery process heightened her resolve to serve others. Once restored to health, she entered public life.

Oklahoma was an interesting place to be a leader. The Cherokees confronted intense social and economic problems, just as other Oklahomans did. The Vietnam War heightened political concerns across the entire political spectrum, and even as it was winding down, domestic tensions flared. Mankiller's progressive views were not always congruent with those of her more conservative and pro–Vietnam War neighbors. Merle Haggard, a fellow Oklahoman, sang out his displeasure with all things progressive in "Okie from Muskogee," and the song lingered in the political air of Oklahoma. Haggard's song represented his sense of Oklahoma, a sense embraced by many a conservative Oklahoman. Mankiller would have to navigate through such mutterings. While Haggard and others were protesting the protestors of the Vietnam War, Mankiller was continuing to learn from her community and preparing to lead.

Mankiller knew she needed more formal education in order to help solve the challenges that confronted her community. In the years following her automobile accident she earned a college degree from Stillwell Flaming Rainbow University Without Walls, an institution journalist Chris Brawley described as known "to provide personalized college education for isolated Indians and rural whites in this beautifully treed and poverty stricken section of the state."

Her alma mater has since closed, but its ideas were certainly kept alive through Mankiller's community contributions. A "university without walls" seems like a fitting metaphor for Mankiller's continual quest for knowledge, a quest that empowered her and the many she served. Mankiller's knowledge began with books. She grew up with no television or electricity, so reading books provided a good base for the informed leader she came to be. The following excerpt from a letter dated April 14, 1993, that she wrote to the dean of the University of Oklahoma Library illustrates her understanding of community and schooling, an understanding that was as expansive as the geography of Oklahoma:

> Reading introduced me to a world beyond my small rural Oklahoma community. By reading I learned about all kinds of people and places. I was able to learn that people with very different lifestyles had similar concerns and sometimes similar hopes for the future.

Several books have had a profound effect but none more than a 1978 reading of Paolo Freire's "Pedagogy of the Oppressed." Freire's clear description of oppressed peoples' view of themselves and the world around them dramatically altered the way I view community development work.

Mankiller continued, explaining that reading still played a central role in her life. Her varied and expansive reading list included selections from Pulitzer Prize winners, philosophers, feminists, and more. She emphasized the importance of reading amid the business of everyday life. "Reading is a common and endeared activity for community members of the Great Plains," she wrote. "If a student is asked about the important educational activities in their Great Plains place, reading is often listed as the favorite. The Carnegie library is a physical mainstay of Great Plains communities." Mankiller recognized the need for greater educational infrastructure and for transforming her words into action.

Delivering Water

Mankiller began her perhaps most famous campaign with a simple vision: to supply clean water to Cherokee communities. Her effort is vividly captured in the 2013 film *The Cherokee Word for Water*. In the 1980s Mankiller was the community development director for the Cherokee town of Bell, which, like many Cherokee communities of the time, had no running water. Mankiller led a community-based effort to build a pipeline that would supply water to Bell and other towns along its path. During the process she learned important lessons on the politics of empowerment and community development. According to observers, the efforts were gadugi (working together), a guiding principle in Mankiller's method of leadership. Still, Mankiller was the driving force from start to finish, demonstrating unwavering determination, perseverance, and commitment to the greater good.

Mankiller worked *with*, not above, her fellow community members. She toiled shoulder-to-shoulder at the most basic level, digging trenches and laying pipe. When not engaged in manual labor, she served as her own public relations director, often bringing the project to a larger Oklahoman and national audience. In the midst of all this work, Mankiller remained a dedicated mother, her actions strongly suggesting that political life starts with family and only then moves into and throughout the community.

In this early project, Mankiller developed a pragmatic appreciation of the connections between community and government. She came to realize that cynical attitudes toward government provide no cure for community ills. While Mankiller was at times rightly critical of government and a strong advocate for community members, she knew how to work *with* and not *against* government. She could see the advantages of obtaining government grants and persuading the greater public of the benefits of the water project.

Not everyone supported her as she navigated through community issues and passions. Skeptics, disinterested bureaucrats, and even fellow Cherokees expressed misgivings, and some believed leadership on this scale was not appropriate for a woman. But she refused to be intimidated by naysayers, remarking in *The Cherokee Word for Water*, "I learned a long time ago that I can't control the challenges the creator sends my way, but I can control the way I think about them and deal with them." Mankiller clearly believed in herself. Government is a given, but individuals make the true differences in and out of government. Mankiller saw the need to take part in the formal political process, even though political combatants would from time to time get their licks in on her. She did not wilt.

Mankiller's political savvy provides a model for those interested in understanding the relationship between community building and leadership. There are numerous so-called leadership institutes and schools, and formal organizations tend to prey upon unwitting Great Plains citizens to engage in leadership camps. But there seems to be no substitute for putting words into action as Mankiller did. This historical leader understood from an early age that she was not above others because of her formal education; instead, she aptly connected her accumulation of knowledge to her political actions.

Beyond the Water Endeavor

The Bell project provided Mankiller both the political capital and the confidence to proceed with greater endeavors. Neighbors near and far had felt the positive impact of her leadership. From this successful experience, Mankiller knew she was highly capable and had the potential to lead. She decided to jump into the broader political spectrum.

Mankiller focused next on leading the entire Cherokee Nation, but obstacles abounded. First and foremost, she was a woman. Despite her achievement in bringing water to communities, the Cherokee electorate seemed reluctant to have a woman as its principal chief. They had fewer objections to a woman being vice chief, and Mankiller served in that role for Chief Ross Swimmer beginning in 1982. Even then, the road was not easy. Policy in this area was set by a federal court case, *Wheeler v. Swimmer* (1987), which reaffirmed tribal political autonomy. R. Perry Wheeler had hoped to be chief rather than Swimmer, and he attempted to employ federal law to remove Swimmer; however, the court held that Cherokee law prevailed. Thus Swimmer became the principal chief. But three years later Swimmer left his position to take a job in the Reagan administration.

Mankiller thus rose to principal chief by default. This complex chain of events illustrates Mankiller's persevering political will. She navigated the political maze to her advantage, and in turn, she gained a position from which to serve her fellow Cherokees. Once the path was open, Mankiller was able to lead according to her vision. Her accomplishments and endearing personal style allowed her to gain considerable trust and, in turn, popularity. She was elected principal chief in her own right in 1987 and reelected in 1991.

The late 1980s and early 1990s were packed with economic and social issues. At the national level, Mankiller had to navigate President Reagan's nationwide agenda of reducing support for social programs. Locally, Oklahomans were coping with a drastic drop in oil prices. Mankiller knew well that she had to partner with other governmental entities within Oklahoma and on the federal level. For example, she worked to bring hydroelectric power through the development of dams by coupling Cherokee electricity needs with the needs of Oklahomans generally. Building dams confronted Mankiller with some interesting and nuanced theoretical arguments. The Cherokees' view of nature as sacred, so often a guide for the nation, might argue against any dam construction, but dams brought undeniable economic opportunities to the Cherokees. Mankiller's approach as usual was pragmatic, and she used her political skills effectively to allay her constituents' environmental concerns.

Improvement of Cherokee life was the driving force for Mankiller. In 1985 the *Courier-Mail* quoted Mankiller as she described governing the Cherokee Nation: "Major issues are poverty, health and education. We have the same problems the state has." She went on to explain that Oklahoma had relied too heavily on oil and agriculture. As head of the nation's second-largest and one of its most progressive Indian tribes, Mankiller, according to Michael Vazquez from the *Huffington Post*, believed she was championing the cause of the poor. Mankiller advocated for gift shops and dams and everything in between. The Cherokee and larger Oklahoma economies were interrelated, and Mankiller wanted financial benefits to be felt in Cherokee communities. She embraced partnerships with Oklahoma governmental entities, if her community benefited. In simple cost-benefit terms, she calculated the best interest of those she served, and the result drove her decisions.

Her style of leadership is vividly illustrated in a directive that she sent to her executive director regarding cigarette licensing, found in her archives:

> Would you please convene the appropriate people from business and community development to put together criteria and a plan for licensing smoke shops for non-profit, community-based organizations? I don't care how you do it or how discriminatory it sounds but I want these licenses to go primarily to full-blood Cherokees in rural poor communities who are doing real work. It will be a little harder to do this work but getting money to those communities is a priority. If the Creeks and Navajos can find a mechanism to get money to their chapters and communities, so can we. We need to get together as soon as possible and sketch some preliminary guidelines then convene a meeting with the Council to get their input. Tribally operated smoke shops are not prohibited and we should proceed on those that are nowhere near a distinct Cherokee community of any kind. Please keep me posted.

While smoking tobacco is indeed harmful to health, Mankiller understood the benefits of economic profits. In 1986 the *New York Times* described Mankiller's pragmatic orientation. It reported that after she was sworn in as chief, one of her main priorities was to create a stable economy by attracting "responsible businesses" of whatever variety. "Unemployment continues to be 'the single most serious problem,'" Mankiller stated. The article described her proactive approach to the unemployment issue by noting the partnership she created between the Cherokee Nation, the Southwestern Power Association, and the Army Corps of Engineers.

The Arkansas River was, and still is, a very important part of Cherokee land, and ownership of the riverbed was an essential component of Cherokee control of that land. The river held potential for developmental possibilities. During Mankiller's watch, in *United States v. Cherokee Nation of Oklahoma* (1987), the U.S. Supreme Court decided in favor of the Cherokees, granting title of the riverbed to the tribe. The impact of this case is enduring. Mankiller interpreted nature in terms of the Cherokee culture—land and water are sacred, hardly commercial. Yet she also understood the pragmatic implications that flowed from ownership of the riverbed. Simply put, ownership brought control over a variety of commercial possibilities. She merged the Native ideal with the pragmatism of ownership, time and time again incorporating Cherokee traditions with the political will to bring a better life for her people. Her pragmatic philosophy delivered real economic benefits, none more visible than the Arkansas River dam project near Bell, Oklahoma. The hydroelectric power plant associated with the Arkansas River dam generated electricity and economic opportunities. But her approach was to stimulate many varieties of economic activities, believing the Cherokees could partner with many others to produce a stable economy. The evidence of her success was noted, as the *New York Times* reported that Oklahoma's unemployment rate had improved to 8 percent in 1986.

Despite her skills, Mankiller was not successful in achieving all her goals, even when solutions were evident to her. On the societal front, Mankiller was not afraid to call out Oklahoma policymakers when her fellow Cherokees and others were harmed by state government rules and regulations. In its schools, Oklahoma was not always inclusive in opening opportunity to all. For example, the state continued to operate segregated graduate programs, finally outlawed by the U.S. Supreme Court in *McLaurin v. Oklahoma State Regents for Higher Education* (1987). Mankiller confronted many other anticommunity policies in the state's education system. Often she encouraged others to speak up. An appeal in a February 1993 letter to one of her community members, Merry C. Sunday, regarding ongoing racial segregation and possible discrimination in higher education illustrates the urgency she felt:

> As Chief of one of the biggest tribes in the nation, and since the state of Oklahoma boasts of its high Indian population, who better to keep a watchful eye of the outcome of this issue, especially since it involves a tribal member. Who knows how many Higher Education Scholarship recipients have fallen prey to these types of educational practices. It is time we take notice and begin monitoring the schools as well. After all, when we send our kids off to school we are investing in our tribe's best resource, our youth. Letters from you to the President of the University of Oklahoma and the Chancellor for Higher Education, in reference to your concern of the allegations in Warren's letter, would have a tremendous impact. You have a vested interest in the welfare of Indian people. You can hold them accountable to their commitment of Affirmative Action (enclosure # 5) like no one else.

Other times Mankiller herself was the advocate. In a letter dated March 3, 1993, to Dr. Richard Van Horn, the president of the University of Oklahoma, and Dr. Hans Brisch, the president of the university's board of regents, Mankiller expresses her belief that it is possible to prove a "pattern of discrimination against minority students." She refers to letters from minority students describing discriminatory situations and shows her interest in the matter by writing, "I have asked that the family keep me informed about the status of their complaint as well as that of any class action suit which may be filed on behalf of former students. As Principal Chief of the Cherokee Nation, I have an obligation to constituents to look at any practices which are or might be damaging to Cherokee students." She concludes the letter by requesting that staff be available to speak with students who have similar complaints. In this case, Mankiller did not prevail, but her advocacy demonstrated her emphasis on education. She knew personally the empowerment that education brings.

Attachment to the Land

Wilma Mankiller understood that an attachment to land often leads to stewardship of that land. She was driven to protect tribal sovereignty, which as she saw it, covered Cherokee land and water as well as people. In a letter to the president of the board of regents and the president of the University of Oklahoma, Mankiller repeats something she was told "decades ago," which is that "tribal sovereignty is a sacred trust." Mankiller relates how their Cherokee ancestors spoke with eloquence about Indian history and culture but how, since the ancestors are gone, they can no longer do so. The missive reveals her deep commitment to advocating for her community: "It then is our duty as Indian people to always remember our responsibility to speak for those who cannot speak for themselves. We have given up way too much. . . . From this day forward we must pledge to not allow any more of our rights to be eroded, we must not be moved a single inch, not a single inch."

The land was sacred, and the working of the land provided empowerment for the Cherokee people. Mankiller's governing embraced the sacred and the pragmatic possibilities of land and work.

Cooking as a Governing Metaphor

Mankiller's ability to find harmony through blending traditional Cherokee values with pragmatic possibilities found a parallel in her culinary skills. As John Snowden, my beloved law professor at the University of Nebraska, said, we should govern as we cook fish; cooking fish or nearly any item well requires great care. The lessons for good governing are abundant. Beverly Cox, an author who writes on Native American topics, says that while most people remember Mankiller as an "author, activist, and the first female principal chief of the Cherokee Nation," she was also a great cook who enjoyed entertaining at her home in Oklahoma. Cox observes that the chief as chef also made the connection. In her cookbook *The Chief Cooks*, Mankiller writes, "I am not a natural cook, but instead a cultivated one. I appreciate good food and the nurturing it represents. I know also that cooking brings the happiness and warmth synonymous with home and family so important in Cherokee culture and, as in my job as chief, I believe in blending and adapting to new ways while keeping the old ones always with us."

Cooking is an apt metaphor for the way in which Mankiller governed. Her profound appreciation of place allowed her to utilize the best of the past, but this appreciation also allowed her to improve upon prior collective strengths, blending old and new ways. Her political skills are important to identify and emulate as a governing example for the Cherokees and for others interested in entering politics to build community of the Great Plains. Her many contributions are important for those attracted to sustaining life in this particular territory. Mankiller's influences are summarized in House Resolution 1237 (2010), which honored her at the time of her death:

Whereas Wilma was formally elected to serve as the first female Principal Chief of the Cherokee Nation in 1987 and was overwhelmingly re-elected in 1991; Whereas during her time as Principal Chief, Wilma focused on education and health care, overseeing the construction of new schools, job-training centers, health clinics, community development, and award-winning housing and water projects in low-income communities; Whereas over the course of her three terms, Wilma made great strides to reinstate the traditional Cherokee culture and values, especially the role of women, reinvigorating the Cherokee Nation through community development projects where men and women work collectively for the common good.

Mankiller's life story serves notice to interested community builders: building community is no simple task, and Mankiller's political devotion exacted a heavy personal price. In a letter to a single mother, Mankiller advised her not to take on another job, given that she already worked long hours and had the additional responsibility of being both a mother and a father to her children. "I believe that love, attention, and time spent with children is far more important than any extra things you may be able to buy them," Mankiller wrote. "If I had to do anything over again, I would spend more time with my children. . . . It seems like I had them for such a little amount of time."

Balancing family and political life challenged Mankiller, as happens with many community leaders. They understand that spectators do very little to improve community life, but the personal price is often high and the impact might not be obvious. This undercurrent caused Mankiller to lament on her life in a letter to Doris Raper in July 1993, "As I grow older and lose more of my friends, this Blackfoot quotation means more to me: 'What is life? It is the flash of a firefly in the night. It is the breath of a buffalo in the winter time, it is the little shadow which runs across the grass and loses itself in the Sunset.'"

Mankiller was one such individual who was highly engaged in community politics. Not all she did was upright, but her intention was to make life better for her fellow Cherokees as well as the whole population of Oklahoma. Mankiller's political activities connected good politics and perpetuation of community life.

The benefits of Chief Mankiller's contributions are still present. Her legacy has had a profound impact on the Cherokees, Oklahomans, and all who continue to emulate her actions. The tribe that she held so close to her heart continues to thrive. As the Cherokee tribal website notes, the tribe encompasses more than 317,000 citizens, 8,000 employees, and a variety of "tribal enterprises" in Oklahoma and surrounding areas. The Cherokee Nation's economic impact is more than $1.5 billion annually in these areas, which makes the tribe "one of the largest employers in northeastern Oklahoma" and the "largest tribal nation in the United States." Principal Chief Bill John Baker said in a press release, "The Cherokee Nation is proud to be a vital and lasting part of the fabric of Oklahoma's economy. With a presence in 14 counties throughout northeast Oklahoma, our roots are here and will always be here. We are proud of the progress of a generation and look forward to supporting northeast Oklahoma for generations to come."

Mankiller's work for the common good is an aim that is shared by many, especially many who live on the Great Plains. While there might be disagreement over the particular paths taken to reach this common good, the paths should interest students of politics as well as concerned citizens. The official Cherokee Nation organization website captures the impact Mankiller had on the Cherokees. Acquiring knowledge, whether from books or experiences, was part of Mankiller's life cycle and was embodied in her political life. Her learning took on a social edge in that she knew she was highly capable of making a difference in the lives of others. This was the core of her leadership, and she exerted such knowledge over the years through her active citizenship. She led by example rather than just words. Pulling together her vast knowledge as well as balancing the demands of raising children and later rebounding from a near-fatal car accident, Mankiller understood that leadership should be achieved through one's actions. She was undaunted by skeptics and bureaucratic politics. Bureaucracy, as she well understood, is impersonal and unresponsive to individual claims. The hierarchy of a bureau is achieved by following rules and is constructed for efficiencies; the human factor, which includes a variety of soft variables, can be lost altogether. Mankiller resisted such bureaucratic rigidity; rather, she led from her understanding of working together, gadugi.

Mankiller was also receptive to environmental concerns, as evidenced by the body of her political work. She worked in concert with "mother earth" and did her best to draw from the gifts nature provided to her and her fellow Cherokees. Mankiller's legacy lies in the dense network of relationships she developed while building community on the Great Plains. Sense of place remains an important idea for Cherokees and Oklahomans, and Mankiller's pragmatic politics inspired this sense of place and community for many. The foundation she built provides a political blueprint for building communities on the Great Plains.

CHAPTER 2

Virginia Smith

Beyond the Kitchen

At the time of the writing of this book, the approval rating of members in the U.S. Congress was 11 percent. Yet many individual congressional members from the rural Great Plains have historically held high popularity rankings. The love-hate relationship with Congress has been frequently noted, but it is the behavior of particular members at the local district level that is most interesting and relevant to this book. Political behavior expressed on behalf of communities reflects the qualities of the people of the plains and allows us to understand their culture. Virginia Smith was one political character who captured the essence of Great Plains political culture.

Smith was a highly popular U.S. representative from Nebraska's Third District. Her service from 1974 to 1990 allowed her to share the innate concern she possessed for others. We could easily overlook the political lessons Smith's career offers because she was a predictable Republican from a predictable Republican district. But her political actions provide insights into the type of public service often exhibited and appreciated by the residents of the Great Plains, and her leadership, although often consistent with the partisan ideology of the GOP, grew out of the interests and influences of her rural constituents.

Consciousness of others leads to a vibrant sense of community, and Smith had a keen appreciation of those around her.

3. Virginia Smith, long-serving U.S. representative from rural Nebraska. *Biographical Directory of the United States Congress: 1774–Present.*

The communities she served were the beneficiaries of such awareness. Smith never outwardly manifested anything that would suggest she was a complicated character; rather, she was grounded in her knowledge and in turn tended to the needs of her neighbors. Her knowledge allowed her to pull people into a greater community, a greater common good. The Smith's archives, housed at Love Library on the University of Nebraska–Lincoln campus, provide an abundance of evidence regarding her caring political nature, positive community contributions, and loveable personality. Her career epitomizes the care and concern she held for others, making a natural fit between her and the constituents she served.

A personal encounter with Representative Smith was an early indicator for me of her nature. Sometime in the winter of 1989, my wife and I had just taken our three-year-old son and five-year-old daughter for an evening swim in the indoor basement pool at the Cornhusker Hotel in Lincoln, Nebraska. The four of us, still dripping from the swim, got into the elevator, aimed directly for our bedtime destination. Before the elevator completely shut, a pleasant older woman quietly offered an apologetic "excuse me" and politely entered the elevator. I soon realized that the new passenger was Representative Virginia Smith. People of the Great Plains do not avoid eye contact, and that was the case in the elevator. I profoundly remarked, "Hello. You are Representative Smith!" She affirmed her identity, and we had an enjoyable and thoughtful conversation. Smith gleaned all our names (Sarah, Pete, Diane, Peter) in addition to our address in Kearney. She then managed to rattle off a list of people on our street as well as a long list of my colleagues at the college where I worked, Kearney State College (later to become the University of Nebraska at Kearney). She extended a timeless offer to help if she was ever needed. Had we not been dripping from the swim, I think we would have melted a bit. We exited at our floor, and she continued on her way. I wanted to invite her in for cookies and milk with the kids, but my star-struck trance prevented the words from coming out. I certainly remember our meeting that evening and always will.

Not only is my experience an example of Smith's personal style, but on a grander scale it illustrates the importance of Congress's representative nature when it comes to the people members serve. Potomac fever, a condition that induces members of Congress to love life and actions in Washington so much that they forget their home base, never infected Smith. Richard Fenno, a noted political scientist, wrote of the importance of "home style"—a personal connection nurtured by a particular representative for his or her constituents. Personally knowing your constituents provides a sturdy foundation for service and leadership. The story of Virginia Smith is a story of such governance.

Smith was born in Iowa in 1911 and moved westward for college, attending the University of Nebraska in Lincoln. At the university she met her husband, Haven, and after graduation moved to Chappell, a small but lively town on the western fringes of Nebraska. They bought a wheat farm and, having no children, Smith made wheat farming her primary focus. The political economy associated with wheat would remain an interest throughout her political life. The 1950s was a decade with very few opportunities for women in the Great Plains to engage in broader governmental processes; women were expected to manage the household, not the affairs of the political community. Although the region had many examples of strong women—its famous chronicler was Willa Cather—males continued to dominate politics, and there was limited female participation in community political matters. Still, in parent-teacher associations, church groups, and assorted women auxiliaries, women made their mark, and it is perhaps not surprising that these experiences eventually led to electoral opportunity. Smith decided to enter politics. She honed her political skills, and local community life provided her the opportunity to serve.

In Chappell, as in other thinly populated places, neighbors, regardless of gender or age, were quick to pitch in when extra help was needed. Smith knew her community needed builders of both genders, and she knew she could contribute. A longtime friend and leader of the Buffalo County Republican Party, Tom Tye, said Smith was naturally drawn to politics, and while her gender presented an obvious obstacle, it could be diminished by positive actions. Smith had some positive women political associates nearby: Kay Orr (a Republican) was working her way up to serve as Nebraska's governor, while Helen Boosalis (a Democrat) served as mayor of Lincoln. Undaunted by the gender issues, Smith embarked on her path of political service.

Education: Smith's Open Target

Smith's entrance into politics and the way she earned her first credentials were not all that unusual. She started by participating in several service organizations, which allowed her to build social capital in her community and take incremental steps on a larger political foray. She was active in business and rural-life groups. She became interested in education issues, a benign entry point for her; she developed a greater understanding of the importance of elementary and secondary schooling and the opportunities inherent in having an undergraduate degree. She and Haven later bequeathed scholarships for following generations, and her work in education continues to be felt.

Smith's attentiveness to education was formalized when she was appointed to the Nebraska State College Board in 1950, serving on it for a decade. This community-centered service heightened her awareness of the fact that the Third District usually had to deal with political leftovers. It was far removed from political power in Lincoln, the state's capital, and its citizens often seemed forgotten. The state college system was designed to provide education for rural Nebraskans, and it included four institutions, formerly termed "normal colleges," located in Peru, Wayne, Kearney, and Chadron (the latter two were in Smith's home district). These regional institutions served as small, less comprehensive alternatives to the University of Nebraska, the comprehensive land-grant university. The rural- and teacher-oriented state colleges offered Smith the opportunity to provide effective and strategic leadership, and the mission of the colleges fit nicely with her concern for community. An illustration of this fit can be seen through Smith's later dealings with Kearney State College president William "Bill" Nester, while she served as a congressional representative. Nester wanted then–vice president George H. W. Bush to deliver the Kearney State College commencement address in 1987, and he called upon Smith for help. Despite her pleas, Bush declined the invitation. Smith assured Nester that Bush's decision was not a reflection of the value of Kearney State College, writing in a May 14, 1987, letter, "Despite Vice President Bush's bad judgment declining your invitation, I know your Spring commencement on May 15, 1987 will be wonderful just the same." Smith was always the advocate and often positive even in setbacks.

As an advocate for the empowering possibilities offered through the state colleges, Smith lobbied for the needs of rural Nebraska to statewide populations and policymakers. The impact of her work still lingers. Thousands of education majors graduated from the state college system and then taught and continue to teach in rural schools. Their influence on community life has been great, and Smith's impact, while not always realized or measured, was highly positive. During her time on the state college board she also developed political skills that would serve her well on a larger stage. The experience credentialed Smith to entertain greater service opportunities made possible through election, not appointment. Ultimately, she turned her attention to running for the U.S. House of

Representatives—a position she felt would allow her to better serve the population she admired.

Race to Political Involvement

Smith was chosen as the Republican nominee for Nebraska's Third District in the 1974 election. She had gained the confidence of her party as a loyal Republican who had served as a delegate to the party's national conventions since 1956. Her personal qualities and skill captured the attention of the party organization, and she was seen as a solid candidate to run in 1974. Despite the overwhelming advantage Republicans held in party registrations in the Third District, the race would be highly competitive. Democrats believed they had a good chance to capture the open seat because their support had been growing throughout the Great Plains and because women candidates for political office still faced significant challenges in the 1970s. Despite gender concerns, conservative Nebraska Republicans had accepted Smith, and the party organization hoped she would be a winner. But the election was rough.

The 1974 election was effectively decided by what turned out to be a misstep by Smith's Democratic foe, Wayne Ziebarth, when he declared that "in politics, a woman's role is in the home." While political competition was often harsh on women seeking public office, the rural constituents of the Third Congressional District were not always so severe. In fact, Republicans in rural Nebraska apparently cared less about the gender of a candidate than whether the candidate was honest, hardworking, and dedicated to others. Stereotypes gave way to the reality that Smith, despite her gender, had a place beyond the confines of the kitchen. She had a track record of community involvement. Her record of accomplishment was punctuated in 1974 as she won the election to the Third Congressional District.

Smith, newly elected, now faced the question of what kind of representative she would be. The Third Congressional District is vast by most standards. Containing around sixty-five thousand square miles, it is about the size of Wisconsin and larger than twenty-seven other states. Unlike the First District (Lincoln) and Second District (Omaha), which contain dense populations and airports that make constituent service physically easier, the Third District was extremely challenging. To start, the people of the district, in 1974 and even today, expected personal, face-to-face conversations with candidates. Travel down nearly any state highway in the wide-open Third District and the driver in a passing vehicle will wave with one or two fingers. Those unaccustomed to the signal should practice the "passerby wave," utilizing the correct finger (index) or fingers (index and middle together), or a complete wave. The friendly culture and her interest in getting to know others meant that Smith had a vastly larger "community" to grow close to.

Beyond her constituents' expectation to know her, Smith faced the challenge of distance. Because there are no major airports in the Third District, flights from Washington DC to western Nebraska routed a passenger through Dallas and then Grand Island; direct connections were rarely available. Once in Grand Island, the driving distance between communities is enormous, and relating personally to constituents implied a demanding travel log. Smith committed herself to personal communication, especially face-to-face conversations, and she became famous for her "home style." Her husband, Haven, served as her driver and confidant, driving and listening to Smith exercise representative democracy at its very best.

Smith energetically pursued and utilized resources gained through her position to help Third District communities. She developed the skill to understand the people she served, her foes and friends, and perhaps most importantly, herself. Her personal notes reflect confidence in herself, and her extensive personal records document her growing self-assurance that she could truly assist others. Tom Tye, the chair of the Buffalo County Republicans and one of Smith's strongest supporters, said she was like "everyone's grandmother." It was as if she knew everyone in her district. Based on my experience with her in the Cornhusker elevator, maybe she did.

The years Smith spent in Congress provide insight into her many contributions to communities throughout Nebraska and beyond. Nostalgia may fool one into thinking that the period in which she served was uncomplicated, simpler than the problematic world of today. But Representative Smith was confronted with a variety of issues—some seemingly simple while others decidedly complex. Like many of her Third District constituents, she was a problem solver—a personality trait formed through her profound grounding in the place and people of her rural district.

Connecting Nebraska to the National Government

Smith worked hard, but seemingly without stress, to link her constituents to the national government. They often experienced difficulty in navigating the bureaucracy, and the government in Washington seemed far removed. Smith was able to lower the barriers, perceived or real, between the plains and the nation's capital. For example, shortly after her election, communities across America were preparing for the bicentennial celebration. The rural population in the Great Plains was decreasing despite a strong increase in community spirit. Towns within the Third District, many facing population decline, wanted to join in the celebration of America as well as showcase their particular communities. Smith discovered there was a federal program allowing towns to become official bicentennial communities. She wrote John Werner, administrator of the American Revolution

Bicentennial Administration, time and again, pestering him to support Third District communities. She understood that the bicentennial designation could be especially important to remote communities that often felt neglected and anxious about their futures. The events accompanying Fourth of July celebrations could build local identity and social capital, helpful to the towns' development. Smith's ability to navigate the bureaucracy allowed her to cut the red tape, and her assistance allowed these communities to participate in the national celebration. Many Third District towns celebrated the bicentennial and benefited from the spirit of common purpose.

Not all public affairs were pitched at this less-than-contentious tone. Smith faced real political battles, in which the issues involved were complex and complicated.

Opening Markets

In the period from 1974 to 1990, farm prices were highly variable. While the early 1970s were good for many farmers, prosperity slowly diminished as the 1980s approached. Third District constituents as well as the entire agricultural sector felt despair in the 1980s, as supply out-stepped the market and prices sagged. Smith set to work to find new external markets in the Soviet Union and China for the region's farm products, especially wheat. Her efforts succeeded in opening international markets to Great Plains farmers. Even so, the 1980s economy was less than robust for farmers and their communities. Smith continued her fight within Congress. In 1980 she sent wheat coffee cakes to her colleagues, a political tactic that reinforced her effective communication skills and engaging personality. The personalized letter she included with each cake created heightened interest and support from her colleagues for wheat farmers. Many of her colleagues responded positively to her "coffee cake" communiqué, seeing it as a folksy and effective

Great Plains style. Representatives from the wheat-producing Great Plains and beyond supported her legislative efforts to subsidize the work of fellow wheat farmers.

Her advocacy was in part an act of self-interest—after all, Smith was a wheat farmer herself—but it was also driven by her personal interest in a larger issue: feeding the greater community, especially the hungry. And if feeding the hungry also served her Nebraska constituents, she was happy to live with the coincidence. She welcomed opportunities to partner with entities that aimed to mitigate hunger, as she did with the Multiplication of Loaves Project (MLP), a collaborative effort between churches, the states of Kansas and Nebraska, and the U.S. Department of Agriculture (USDA). At the time, many people were searching for ways to feed those who didn't have the financial means to feed themselves, and many also were searching for ways to help farmers who had experienced sharp declines in income in recent years. In a 1983 letter to Secretary of Agriculture John Block, now held in Smith's archives at the University of Nebraska–Lincoln, Smith describes the MLP as "a distribution system for local churches. The MLP distributed 31 tons of pinto beans, popcorn, cracked wheat, and whole wheat to local churches in the Great Plains." The food came from the surpluses of Great Plains farmers.

The MLP enabled social and religious agencies to partner with the USDA in a manner consistent with the beliefs of Smith and fellow Great Plains people. It recognized that thriftiness often gave pause to those in need, so that many who needed food were reluctant to accept government aid. "In Nebraska, for example," noted Father Jogues Epple, an Episcopalian priest and MLP leader, "less than half of those eligible for FSP [the Food Stamp Program] apply for the USDA's food stamps." The program also stressed frugality, an approach accepted by Smith and espoused by the larger rural community. Explaining that "Great

Plains frugality describes the traditional approach for feeding the weak," Epple observed that "the innovative approaches represented by [the MLP] Proposal can put people to work feeding themselves at the discretion of the [USDA] Secretary."

For Smith, mitigating hunger was simply part of taking care of community members and building a communal foundation. It also allowed Smith to work with others beyond the Third District, notably Kansas senators Nancy Kassebaum and Bob Dole (both Republicans) and Nebraska senators J. James Exon and Edward Zorinsky (both Democrats). Together they persuaded the USDA to support Multiplication of Loaves. Smith's leadership and ability to work with a diverse set of policy makers displayed her skill in finding common ground for the community good. The elements of volunteering and limited government incorporated in the project seemed consistent with her partisan Republican free-market orientation, and its use of market excess provided relief for the real issue of hunger. This endeavor showcased her understanding of the generous spirit of the people in her community, but most importantly, it also brought food to hungry people. This latter aspect transcended partisanship and more aptly reflected the neighborly care so often found in the rural communities of the Great Plains.

Smith reconciled her lobbying for the federally funded Multiplication of Loaves with her partisan Republican ideology of small government by advocating for private initiatives to take the first lead, and seeing government support as following in a cooperative manner. Her support for the project illustrates a care and concern for others but not necessarily a truly free social giving of food. Caring for others, in this view, starts at the individual level, a perspective that many in the Great Plains shared. Smith's policy preferences and initiatives balanced individualism with community-based concern for feeding others, with the added bonus that her farmer constituents and other Great Plains farmers would provide the food. These actions were consistent with her constituents' attitudes and with Republican ideology, which held that government social programs had to be coupled with private-sector efforts.

Irrigation Increase: Damming the Niobrara and Calamus Rivers

Smith's mantra was building agricultural opportunity, and she often searched for economic catalysts to increase and perpetuate sustainability in the Third District. One such catalyst was irrigation. Her predecessor, Representative Dave Martin, also thought that water for irrigation was essential for crop production, but his proposal to have numerous dams constructed on the Platte River lacked support from many of his fellow Third District Republicans and ultimately failed. Still, Smith thought it was essential to build dams so that her constituents could have greater economic success.

Nebraska is situated on the Ogallala Aquifer, an immense reservoir of underground water that allows the state to have more irrigated land than any other state in the country. Because underground and surface water are connected hydrologically, water policy to this day is complicated by the need to regulate the underground resource as well as streams and rivers and water held by dams. Water rights are often contradictory and in conflict, spurring frequent litigation. Irrigation has heightened the intensity of water fights. After all, irrigation continues to bring economic prosperity to the farmers of Nebraska. Smith knew well the economic benefits that can come from irrigation, and she and the region's farmers also understood the forces dealt by Mother Nature, including drought, which causes worry to all who live in this region. Even so, such worry did not mean that residents would embrace a pro-dam agenda.

Smith and others believed that more irrigated acres would lead to greater prosperity, and their eyes turned to the Niobrara River and the Calamus River. The Niobrara and Calamus lie roughly three hours north of Nebraska's midpoint, the Interstate 80 corridor that through-travelers are so familiar with. Off the beaten path of interstate travel, the beauty of these rivers is astounding. Ignoring their beauty and remoteness, Smith viewed them as sources of water for irrigators. Dam water, she thought, was good for her constituents and consistent with her political agenda.

Smith prevailed on the Calamus dam effort, so that today the river flows into the large and placid Calamus Reservoir above the dam. But she failed to gain approval for dams on the Niobrara River. Residents' attitudes varied regarding preservation and irrigation, providing mixed political messages for the pragmatic Smith. The dam push, particularly surrounding the Niobrara River, came to be one of the few blemishes on her political career. Her proposals were met with a clear and enduring defeat. The reasons for her defeat are instructive.

Smith's single-minded drive to increase irrigation met with considerable resistance from other Nebraskans and conservationists beyond Nebraska. The proposed Norden Dam would wall the Niobrara River on nearly eighty thousand acres in Keya Paha and Holt Counties in northern Nebraska. The dam would address irrigation needs of farmers and ranchers and at the time, except among Native American populations, there was a tremendous emphasis on "controlling nature" and increasing agricultural production. But critics, including some of Smith's own constituents, viewed the dam as a threat to the environment and of very little economic benefit. In short, this time Smith's cost-benefit analysis failed to match that of her constituents because they perceived the likely harm to the Niobrara River as being too great and the purported financial gain too small.

The economics of more irrigated acres, and in turn of more commodities in a time of depressed markets, provided additional fodder for rejection of the proposed damming of the river.

The political battle, in a broader sense, revealed the diversity of views among Great Plains residents. The shared sense of place took on different meanings, and Smith discovered that the range of values was greater than she had appreciated. Not all in the Third District, or statewide, or across the Great Plains, wanted more irrigated land at the expense of a cherished river.

She had proposed her Norden project at the end of an era of intense dam building in the Great Plains. During the preceding decades, the U.S. Army Corps of Engineers had constructed multiple massive dams on the Missouri as well as smaller dams on the Platte and many other rivers and streams. Increasingly the public was beginning to see the environmental harm that was being done by the dams as well as their benefits, and no other major dams would be built in the region. The political battle that ensued regarding the Norden Dam illustrated that Smith was a determined advocate even when she had misread the public's mind and miscalculated their support for her position. Those who joined her to support damming the Niobrara were opposed by Third District constituents and despised "eastern conservationists." There was a humorous side-tone to *eastern*, as it referred to the urbanites of Omaha and Lincoln. These opponents preferred conservation and recreational activities such as canoeing the Niobrara over further expansion of row-crop farming. Smith was also opposed by the Republican congressman from the First District as well as the Democratic Second District representative. Smith's Niobrara policy push met with serious resistance from Niobrara-area residents, who possessed an even broader commitment to place, especially landowners who lived in the area around the proposed dam.

The *New York Times* and other national media picked up on the threatened beauty of the Niobrara. One *Times* editorial outlined the flaws of Smith's proposed policy and captured the resistance to her proposal. Reporter John B. Oakes wrote that the Norden Dam would destroy the "biological crossroads," a confluence of six distinctly different ecosystems in an area that is rich in varied plant, bird, and animal life. The Nature Conservancy, Oakes wrote, had purchased the Niobrara Preserve land in 1980 for about $11 million. "Nothing like the Niobrara Preserve exists anywhere else in the United States," he wrote. The Niobrara River was designated as a Wild and Scenic River on May 24, 1991.

Despite the designation and the failure of her proposal, Smith's position remained consistent with the views of many of her constituents who lived near the river. Those who supported Smith were more concerned about outsiders coming in and disrespecting the region than actually in favor of more irrigated land. Once those near the river overcame their fear of outsiders, the Niobrara region began hosting a variety of river tourists, and the economic diversification provided new opportunities for the very people Smith had wanted to serve. In hindsight, Smith would have been pleased with the wild and scenic designation. Communities have benefited from the ecotourism dollars that flow through the region, and outsiders have gained a better understanding of why so many share a love for the Great Plains.

Smith's stubborn focus on the dam and her political defeat did not diminish her belief that her constituents needed better economic prospects in order to remain on the land. She championed providing farmers and ranchers with operating loans and lobbied for guarantees that Commodity Credit Corporation (CCC) loans would be available for her constituents. The CCC, founded in 1933, aimed to help producers through "loans, purchases, payments, and other operations, and [by making] available materials and facilities required in the production and marketing of agricultural commodities." Farmers and ranchers, many facing diminishing resources, relied on a sustained borrowing authority from the CCC. The CCC provided financial relief to farmers and, through them, to rural communities. Unfortunately, the CCC suffered in the 1980s, just like the farmers it served. Smith supported the CCC and worked to be its guardian. Any disruption in the flow of loans would have been disastrous for the agricultural sector, and she understood that the very existence of farmers was at stake. Steven V. Roberts reported in the *New York Times* that her tireless advocacy was a leading force in funding to save the CCC, an act that in turn saved many in the agricultural sector who were facing a "desperately serious plight." The CCC remains an important force in maintaining communities in the rural Great Plains today.

Smith recognized the tension between the region's traditional disdain of "big government" and the need for an empowering government. These tensions challenge the ideological genuineness of leaders like Smith, since the rhetorical benefits of small government could not assist small producers. Smith did not operate as a purist, and big government delivered on aid to the agriculture sector. The political identity of the rural plains, and its contradictions, are well represented by Smith's political savvy and flexibility.

Navigating the national scene while at the same time staying true to the identity of her constituents brought interesting twists in Smith's efforts during the Reagan administration. Smith remained loyal to her constituents as well as to her political party.

Keeping Great Plains Roots in the Reagan Years

President Harry Truman signed into law the National School Lunch Program in 1945. It potentially connected hungry children with surplus food from the farming sector of the Great Plains. But, as with any allocation of scarce resources, periodic tensions over apportionments brought about some contentious politics. And for Smith, her lifelong concern for linking food policy and her agricultural constituents came into conflict with her (and President Reagan's) conservative ideology. Reagan's willingness to reduce the government-assisted school lunch program was compatible with the frugal individualism of the Great Plains, but many Great Plains students suffered poverty and hunger.

The K-12 USDA-based school meal programs were scrutinized by many national lawmakers in the 1980s, including Smith and Reagan. Students on the verge of hunger were in desperate need of a hot lunch, given President Reagan's reluctance to direct the USDA to provide balanced, nutritious meals through the school meal programs. Cost reduction was the mantra of the era. Smith shared in the quest for governmental cost savings, and President Reagan and Representative Smith were seemingly in lockstep when it came to the school lunch program.

Smith reconciled her desire for less government with her concern for feeding hungry children by emphasizing local control. Robert Pear of the *New York Times* reported that Smith saw her belief in "less government" as not lessening her concern for the people being served. Individuals expected collective action, just not necessarily collective action through "big government." She argued that "state and local school boards should be given greater control over how school lunch menus fulfill federal nutritional standards." State and local officials, she said, are "far more likely to provide nutritious meals at the lowest possible cost."

Smith's remark was consistent with the thoughts of residents from her quadrant of the plains as well as Republican Ronald Reagan. Local control of the school lunch program, initiated during Smith's and Reagan's tenure in office, has led many rural schools in Nebraska and other Great Plains states to construct greenhouses and maintain gardens to grow their own healthy foods for K-12 students. The balance between big government and individual autonomy is still seemingly maintained. In the meantime, rural students are using their agricultural know-how to produce healthy community snacks. Smith would be well satisfied by the outcome, on balance.

The notion of feeding those in need presents an interesting insight into the balance Smith usually achieved in addressing community needs while emphasizing individual autonomy from undue governmental intrusion and federal help. The legacy of choice in local schools and programs remains embedded in the lunch policies of rural schools today, a reminder of Smith's impact. Republicanism persists and thrives in its own special form throughout the Great Plains, lacking the edgy nature of national politics. Smith's edge was seemingly softened by her intimate knowledge of the constituents she served over the years.

Evidence of this softened edge is her leadership in rural health. The Rural Health Coalition was designed to provide health care for those far removed from urban health centers. Smith supported the coalition's efforts. But her support foreshadowed the ongoing health care shortages found on the rural Great Plains. Health care is a key component of community survival, development, and quality of life. Rural health care has persisted well beyond the efforts of Smith, and communities continue to remain active in maintaining options for their citizens; no easy task. But the work of teams and coalitions provides a framework for good health policy options.

Smith faced a different challenge with the Reagan administration's military buildup. The spaces of the Great Plains, especially the western edge, seemed to Washington military planners an ideal place to stick the nuclear-tipped Missile-eXperimental, better known in the plural as MX missiles. President Reagan, despite claiming to be a fiscal conservative, advocated for enormously increased spending on defense, including funding for MX missiles in the empty quarters of the Great Plains. While most plains residents, including those in Smith's Third District, held positive opinions of President Reagan, they were less than thrilled with the notion of placing nuclear missiles on their beloved land.

Representative Smith, as a purposeful and pragmatic advocate for her constituents, confronted President Reagan with her concerns regarding the MX missiles. She met with the president and his team, the president arguing the need to place missiles in western Nebraska and Smith urging him to locate the missiles outside of her district. Further, Smith, like her fellow residents, was frugal on fiscal matters and hence skeptical about the MX missiles' cost, as she considered the many issues involved. Because Smith was an instrumental player on the House Appropriations Committee, the White House needed her vote. She needed to balance local loyalties against the pressure from President Reagan. Her concerns about location and funding were counterbalanced by Reagan's popularity. The president lobbied intensely for the missile funding, the key to his plan for increased defense as well as his overall strategy to put pressure on the Soviet Union.

Smith engaged in serious study as to whether or not to support Reagan's missile plan. The usually decisive Smith remained undecided in the early phases of the discussion process. Her uncommitted position reflected both the respect she held for her constituents and her partisan support of the president. Her internal political debate drew substantial media interest. The *Washington Post* reported on a conversation between President Reagan and Smith regarding the decision: "His key point,' Smith told the *Post*, "was that unless we support the MX initiative we will be sending the wrong signal to the Soviets. It wasn't a hard sell, but he ended up by saying, 'I hope I can count on your support.'" Reporter George C. Wilson wrote that Air Force general George Miller, an acquaintance of Smith's, called her after she spoke with the president. Wilson reported that Smith expressed concern to Miller that antiballistic missiles might be deployed near her district to protect the Dense Pack formation of MX missiles just across the Nebraska border outside Warren Air Force Base near Cheyenne, Wyoming. "He [Miller] said it was extremely unlikely that this would happen," Smith stated, "certainly not in the near future."

Smith also received calls from Richard DeLauer (Reagan's undersecretary of defense for research and engineering), who delivered a "low-pressure pitch," according to Wilson, and from Vice President George Bush, who "topped off the administration's lobbying of Smith" and said, "I'm not going to use the term bargaining chip for the MX, but it is an important aid to the arms control negotiations." When Smith was asked how she would vote after the lobbying efforts, Wilson wrote, she responded that she "has more cows than people in her district" and that "There's been a change in [the Third] district. There is now a feeling that we're putting more into defense than we should. People feel there is too much waste. I'm not sure how I will be voting."

Smith ultimately did vote in favor of Reagan's MX missile plan. Her vivid description of her district with "more cows than people" helped give a visual to the sense of place held by constituents of the area, who had trouble discerning the missile plan's benefits. Ultimately, her vote represented a careful balancing, with an ample dose of partisan loyalty.

Smith possessed many characteristics that were shared by her rural plains constituents, including frugality, modesty, and humility. They often led her to a pragmatic position on policies, repeatedly voting as her home district would wish. She understood the fabric of her communities. Not surprisingly, Smith's frugality led her to resist congressional pay raises. The *Washington Post* reported that she introduced legislation to block the 1987 proposed congressional pay raise from $77,400 a year to $89,500 a year, and she also proposed rolling back a 3 percent increase members had received on January 1 of that year. "We can get by on $75,100," the *Post* reported her saying in a one-minute speech. "And overwhelmingly the people back home in my district expect us to. For Nebraskans, times are harsh."

Smith's commitment was to serve others without self-gain. Her behavior in Washington was no different from how she acted in Chappell, Nebraska. She knew not to be two-faced; she understood her place and duty to the people. Smith understood how to lead and make positive impacts on the like-minded residents of the Third District. Her opposition to a pay raise solidified her camaraderie with her constituents.

Smith continuously demonstrated her understanding of people and place on the rural Great Plains. This understanding provided her with confidence to be true to herself and to her constituents, remaining comfortable in her own skin. Like so many of her constituents, she was unpretentious. Her persona fit the rural residents in the communities she served. She became a trailblazer for women, who were then rare in the House of Representatives. Her leadership caught the attention of the national press, although her Nebraska style was surprising for the pundits. In an article about women of the House, the *Washington Post* provided a glimpse of the person: "If there is any difference in the institution from its early days, it is that women are now firmly part of it. They are no longer a curiosity, as they were on the day a decade ago that Virginia Smith, then a representative from Nebraska, hurried from the beauty shop to the floor to vote, still in pink curlers." Smith was an unpretentious advocate of her rural Great Plains base. Voting while wearing pink curlers was of no concern to her.

Smith seriously engaged rural Nebraskans and other rural residents throughout the Great Plains. The farmwife from Chappell made a positive mark on so very many. At the close of her political life, in 1998, Smith was honored as a Nebraska Woman of Distinction. Reporting on the honor, the *Lincoln Journal Star* highlighted her contributions:

Served the Third District from 1974 to 1990.

Led efforts to establish the House Rural Health Care Coalition to work for better medical care in rural areas.

Established a bill that raised the limit on gross farm assets taxable under federal inheritance law.

Smith's home style and plainspoken leadership offer valuable lessons for Great Plains residents. Her actions were patently genuine and her commitments enduring, suggesting that deep understanding of one's constituents is key for community leaders who wish to persist in the rural and often forgotten areas of the plains. Her sense of obligation to civic and community well-being is worth replicating, and indeed, many rural communities depend upon such leadership to survive. Community-minded people who understand the value of place are essential for making the political process work and for building the good life in the Great Plains. Virginia Smith epitomized that autonomous spirit.

Plains people love their land and the residual autonomy provided by wide-open spaces. Yet they are also by and large community oriented, and they are quick to lend a helping hand to neighbors. Commitment to community may conflict with notions of individualism, producing a complex, sometimes contradictory identity. Individualism often leads to an association with the Republican Party, and so the partisan sympathies of the plains are politically red. Yet the region's identity also reflects a community-minded spirit, a generous orientation. Virginia Smith shared this complex nature. The manifestations of these community-minded individualists sustain life on the rural Great Plains. As "everybody's grandmother," Smith had an impact that remains in many rural communities of the Great Plains today.

CHAPTER 3

Junius Groves

From Slave to Potato King

Wilma Mankiller and Virginia Smith demonstrated how electoral politics and political leadership contributed to community life. The two were not primarily motivated by winning elections; rather, they wanted to lift the lives of others in their communities. The Kansas farmer Junius Groves shared the community-building mode of Mankiller and Smith. Aristotle observed that good politics can provide a good life. In the case of the Great Plains, communities are shaped by the natural areas that surround them and by a generous human spirit. Concern for others demonstrates the best of community life. Individuals play a crucial role in imagining and mobilizing for a better future.

Understanding people and the attractions of place are difficult to measure yet easier to appreciate. Political scientists are fond of using aggregate data to make bold statements about the past and future, but we can also extract valuable lessons from the lives of positive leaders. The discovered insights reveal enduring values beneficial to community life. There are ways to serve one's community besides holding elective office. Junius Groves was never elected to office, but nonetheless he was a significant community builder. He is known for making numerous contributions to the civic and social life of African Americans throughout Kansas, yet not much has been written about his personal life or his related community influences.

That he achieved so much, given that his moment in history was infected with open racism directed at African Americans, is remarkable. Those like Groves who navigated through challenges brought by racism reveal new dimensions in the Great Plains spirit of community.

Overcoming the Effects of Slavery and Discrimination

Kansas was in many ways shaped by slavery and pre–Civil War politics. The rush to settle the territory created what was aptly described as "Bleeding" or "Bloody" Kansas. This initial nasty settlement originated from the Kansas-Nebraska Act of 1854 (the act that nullified the Missouri Compromise of 1820 and opened the Kansas territory to a trickle of uneasy settlers). "Popular sovereignty"—the doctrine that each new state could decide for itself whether it would permit slavery or not—was the guiding principle of the day. Proslavery and antislavery settlers poured in, their interactions often turning violent and bloody while Kansas made its decision about whether to permit slavery. In due course, Kansas achieved statehood in 1861 as a nonslave state after the eleven Confederate states left the Union.

African Americans such as Junius Groves migrated to Kansas in search of opportunities. They migrated with hope, aspiration, and some trepidation. While many Kansans extended the welcome mat for new settlers, lawmakers were not so hospitable: They passed a number of laws and policies formally entrenching discrimination toward African Americans, women, and Native Americans. Even in the twenty-first century, the impact of discrimination and prejudice lingers throughout the state as well as within other jurisdictions in the Great Plains. As community building is still in process, residents of the Great Plains continue to be confronted with racial issues.

In the nineteenth century, Kansas, much like other Great Plains states, was viewed as a place of opportunity. As the

4. Junius Groves, "Potato King" and community builder. General Research and Reference Division, Schomburg Center for Research in Black Culture, New York Public Library, Astor, Lenox, and Tilden Foundations.

nineteenth century closed, African Americans fleeing racial violence in the South sought out a better life in Kansas. History would provide an account of misdeeds and missteps, and race issues were just one more challenge to overcome as the newly freed citizens searched for social, political, and economic opportunities. Junius Groves was one of many who embraced the chance to settle in Kansas.

Groves left Kentucky and set out on his journey with other former slaves at his side. What he found was that the demographics in Kansas were not unlike settlement patterns elsewhere in the Great Plains, especially in cities, where racial communities were segregated despite emancipation. Groves had no interest in living under segregation, and he found the African American area of Kansas City particularly distasteful. Instead, he looked to rural life to provide opportunity. The settlement pattern of former slaves resulted in a clustering of rural African American communities, ultimately creating local societies that were also not integrated. But as Joyce Groves Holland, great-granddaughter of Junius Groves, noted, when it came to rural settlement, her great-grandfather always strived for fully integrated communities. In the eyes of Groves and others, rural Kansas was more attractive and less complicated than the urban sites. These settlers soon found that the plains boasted rich, fertile land, but nature, especially weather, could be harsh. Groves and others believed, despite the known challenges, that they could build viable communities and thriving farms and business enterprises. They saw examples of success, for the landscape of the Great Plains was already dotted with successful farm operations, including many black farmers.

According to Anne P. W. Hawkins, in the period 1888 to 1920 there were four thousand African American farmers in Kansas. In the last quarter of the nineteenth century, African Americans began to view farming in Kansas as an opportunity to build economic prosperity and a decent civil life. African American migrants from the South showed sustained interest in Kansas. They founded a number of communities, including most famously Nicodemus, described by the National Park Service as "the only remaining western town established by African-Americans during the Reconstruction period following the Civil War and [which] represents a largely untold story of the western expansion and settlement of the Great Plains." Other African American settlements, like the town of Votaw, thrived but later failed, falling victim to the harsh natural realities of the plains; floods ultimately drove the settlers out of town, according to Marvin Moss. Farmers, regardless of race, were at the mercy of the natural forces operating in the Great Plains.

Groves and other black settlers were able to build communities despite the menacing floods, tornadoes, drought, heat, blizzards, and pests. They left the harsh forces of slavery, a dreadful system created by humans, to forge opportunities in Kansas. But forces of nature are part of one's place, and the sense of belonging expressed by Groves's great-granddaughter is vital to creating community, which is a unifying sense of place.

According to Robert Park, commenting in the *Annals of the American Academy of Political and Social Science* in 1913, Groves was "one of the most successful farmers in the state of Kansas." Park recalls how Groves was born a slave in Kentucky and in 1879, after the war, migrated to Kansas, where he raised potatoes on six acres of a rented farm. By 1913, Park writes, "he now owns 503 acres in the Kaw Valley upon which he raised last year a crop of 55,000 bushels of potatoes." In just a couple of sentences, Park sums up the success and resilience of Junius Groves. He continues by telling how Groves's educated sons, who studied at the Kansas Agricultural College, helped him apply "scientific methods to his farming operations." By doing so, Groves was "able to raise his maximum yield on a single acre to 395 bushels." Park quotes a writer from the *Country Gentleman* describing Groves's new "handsome modern house" as a "twenty-two room palace overlooking a 503 acre farm."

Groves walked from Kentucky to Kansas in search of the American Dream. Starting as a line worker in a meatpacking house, he ultimately landed as a laborer on "Mr. Williams' Farm." Working and saving, Groves forged forward with great success. He ultimately found his spouse, Matilda, and although they wished to marry quickly, they had to wait because he did not have enough money to pay the Kansas marriage fees. So he worked and saved every penny he earned. By farming during the season and in other seasons chopping and selling wood, Groves was eventually able to pay the required fees. He and Matilda could then build their family as well as a community in which to prosper.

"The Groves had 14 children, 12 surviving, who were educated and worked on the 500 acre potato farm," Tisa Anders writes. "The family farm was a world leader in potato production and in 1906 Junius was given the title of 'Potato King of the World.'" At one point, according to his great-granddaughter Joyce Holland, Groves and his wife built a ballroom and roller-skating rink so that their children would stay close to home and not stray into the city. Groves proved to be an extremely successful potato grower, resulting in his ability to provide jobs to a good number of farm employees. His global connections to Mexico and Canada were impressive, and the Union Pacific Railroad built a track just to and from his farm. Other farmers did not always appreciate his success, according to Holland. Rather than prolong a confrontation, Groves, in his philanthropic manner, would give away his crops to those who were hungry. This sent a clear message to other farmers to cooperate and do well for those in more need than themselves.

As Groves turned his efforts to community building, he chose an unlikely pairing of projects: golf and church. He was active in both, but more importantly, both activities were his means to build what today we would call social capital. Leading political scientist and social theorist Robert Putnam reminds us that "bowling alone" provides little social capital; one does not build community through individual isolation. Communities need triggers that pull people together. Further, Putnam asserts based on his data, churchgoers are "nicer" than nonchurchgoers in terms of community involvement—they engage in more activities. Putnam's observations seem to apply nicely to Groves's community leadership.

Drive the state or provincial and local highways either north to south or east to west through the Great Plains and you will find that most communities contain multiple churches in addition to a golf course on the outskirts of town. In stretching Putnam's notion of "bowling alone" to cover golf, we can see that playing golf with friends and family or playing in golf leagues brings people together in greater community. Playing golf alone is contrary to the communitarian spirit of the plains.

Groves was credited with establishing one of the first golf courses for African Americans. He knew how to pull the community together, and his mechanism of choice was recreation. In his case and that of other settlers, playing golf in and of itself had no real benefit; the benefit was in strengthening the bonds of community life.

Groves also played a leading role in anchoring his community when he founded Pleasant Hill Baptist Church in Edwardsville, Kansas. The church is now located across the street from where it was originally built in 1882. Mary Kimbrough (Groves's great-grandniece, whose mother was a Groves) relayed that the generous spirit of Junius Groves remains a part of the church. Among many other things, the church continues to operate a free store through which items such as clothing, appliances, and other essentials are given to those in need. Putnam emphasizes that churches provide yet another essential outlet for community building. It is likely that Groves established the church not for his personal well-being but rather for the well-being of his community. As Kimbrough stated, Groves was a religious man but his main interest was in doing "God's work." He turned theory into practice, building social capital through his engaged involvement in the community, going well beyond the family. Groves, who would not have recognized the term, nonetheless became a clever builder of community social capital when he constructed his golf course and established his church.

In discussions with Holland and Kimbrough, they reported that Groves's golf course, located next to the church near Ninety-Fifth and Fourth Streets in Edwardsville, was eventually turned over for residential development. Still, the effort at recreational development illustrates the importance of gathering and the understanding that individual toil is not enough to satisfy and maintain community life. Holland added that Groves was successful in convincing Kansas City officials to integrate Swope Park. As the area became more integrated, there was no need for a strictly African American golf course. Recreation with others, similar to "bowling in leagues," helped to establish community.

Groves apparently understood that a golf course can serve as a social force for community members, as their coming together through recreation tends to build community. Volunteers frequently help maintain the typical Great Plains golf course. Food and beer are consumed while golfing, and conversations about community life remain lively in the process. Reporter John Paul Newport wrote about the golf course as a force in community life in the *Wall Street Journal*, describing a rural golf course in a Kansas community with a shrinking population surrounded by diminishing family farms. The local high school had fifteen students, and the state golf championship included only thirty-six players from fifteen schools. Newport quoted Bob Becker, a local resident: "It's a hard living out here. The nearest Wal-Mart, and I guess that's the gauge, is 70 miles away. We educate the kids well, so they can go off to the city or to college and get good jobs, but there's not much work here to bring them back." Becker, Newport added, was "proud that a good many have golf skills to take with them. 'Our kids can easily hold their own with the city kids. All they have to learn is the grass-green part.'"

It would be an overreach to conclude that golf is the sole indicator of involvement in Great Plains communities. Along with other social opportunities, however, golf encourages community investment. The building of social capital through golf and other triggering social activities might seem trivial, but as towns in the rural Great Plains struggle to sustain themselves, social options encourage investment in a community. Junius Groves was aware that his fellow residents needed more than hard work to maintain community life.

Groves's success was remarkable given the civic and social restraints he confronted, and many recognized this fact. Once slavery was removed, he showed what the ideal of freely pursuing life, liberty, and happiness could mean in practice. The mere opportunity to work the land despite the foreboding natural forces arrayed against him was sufficient.

The racial oppression of slavery was perpetuated by such later legal constructs as Jim Crow laws, grandfather clauses, segregation policies, poll taxes, and other devices. Yet discrimination seemingly failed to diminish Groves's hopes and aspirations. He appeared particularly skilled at navigating political and ecological forces in order to build a sense of community for his family and neighbors. Kansas was his land of opportunity. Through his newfound freedom and tireless work, Groves, as a new claimant to the American Dream, was able to shape his life and improve the lives of his family members as well as others. His accomplishments demonstrate the positive potentials that come from building communities on the Great Plains. Indeed, his undertakings continue to inspire others. In a PBS series about Groves, one of his descendants notes, "Hearing this story about an ancestor building the 'American Dream' right out of slavery gives me a sense of pride, belonging, and importance that I might not have had if my mother did not keep her father's stories alive."

The sense of belonging as expressed by Groves was vital to his discovery of opportunities in the Great Plains. Community building is fortified when political actions are combined with an appreciation of place.

Groves's path to success began with his individual determination, and his political contributions were generated from involvement in his community, but not in any electoral sense. Electoral success is but one measure, partial at best, of overall contribution to community life; indeed, most who contribute to a community do so outside of electoral politics. They nonetheless contribute to the community's quality of life.

Securing the "American Dream"

Groves's achievements are found in family, work, community, and church. The normative measures of good community politics are understood by the soft values of social well-being, economic empowerment, and overall civic engagement. In these categories Groves attained a high level of success and served as a role model for subsequent generations.

Lessons from Groves's life remain relevant to the puzzle of keeping the Great Plains vital. Farming brought settlers to Kansas, and the economic benefits they achieved provided a real basis to stay on the plains. Community building requires economic rights as well as a degree of social capital. Groves certainly understood the path to economic prosperity, but more importantly for perpetuating life on the Great Plains, he understood the need to build community. The building blocks of community survival come from the multiple factors involved with social capital. Groves's contributions provide hopeful lessons regarding resiliency and the building of community. Great Plains residents develop a sense of community through collective spirit, and Groves put his individual accomplishments aside to build his community. His political style drew on his ability to benefit from his resources as well as social capital; in turn, he displayed how to build community.

Political scientists are fond of discussing the multiple variants that contribute to social capital. But one does not need to be formally trained in political science to understand the relationship between a vibrant community and social capital. If one were to visit with patrons of a local diner, shoppers at a family-run grocery store, churchgoers, or even players out on a golf course, one would quickly learn that active citizens make a huge difference in a community's quality of life. Groves knew how to develop a good life. Perhaps the discord of national politics could be diminished by lessons learned from his example about the importance of working with others in social, economic, and political affairs.

Groves's political world, like that of many on the rural plains, started with family and mushroomed out to the community. In discussions with Groves's great-granddaughter, Joyce Groves Holland, she emphasized that his work almost always related to these two factors of family and community. Of course, this seems to fit with the political character found throughout the plains. Groves preferred the rural Great Plains over urban settings, because he thought the urban environment failed to promote community. He truly believed that community life was best in rural Kansas.

The model of community building established by Junius Groves is still unfolding in the life of African American farmers. Groves and the settlers who followed him provide remarkable lessons regarding the importance of steadfast leadership and resolve in order to develop good political life in communities. Decades later, the dream to settle the Kansas plains remains throughout the African American community.

The town of Nicodemus, Kansas, serves as a reminder of the power that individuals can develop in their place of residence. Nicodemus today is the home of Promised Land Flour, a product that came from the work of five African American wheat farmers. In the year 2000 these farmers started the Nicodemus Flour Co-op, which sells flour to be used in pancake mix. Pancake mix and politics? Yes, a community pancake feed pulls people together—just as Wilma Mankiller's pumpkin pie or Virginia Smith's wheat coffee cake did. The people of the plains know how to gather and in turn know how to govern in community. The Nicodemus community hosts the annual Nicodemus Homecoming Celebration, where the Nicodemus Flour Co-op offers a free pancake breakfast. The co-op also offers its mix in a two-pound decorative sack; all you have to do is "just add water and steady yourself for some good eating and lots of praise from your folks." Such an approach, part of the Great Plains culture, is a great tactic in reaching the political realm.

While the life of Junius Groves illustrates the positive contributions made by former slaves to overall community life on the Great Plains, it would be a mistake to conclude that the experiences of African American farmers on the Great Plains were uniformly positive. Rachel Wolters's poignant article "As Migrants and Immigrants" serves as an important reminder that not all stories were encouraging, as systematic and governmental manifestations of racism were typical on the North American Plains. This racism among farmers has presented persistent challenges in the settlement of the area. Racism on the Great Plains—in both the United States and Canada—did not, however, extinguish the African American will to build community, and black settlers "never lost sight of the importance of a unified black identity and strong familial relationships through chain migrations and valuable exchanges."

The lessons from Groves's life strongly suggest that essential elements of community building include economic opportunities coupled with strong social capital. Groves was not an elected leader, but he certainly understood the importance of leading and building community life. The beauty of the Great Plains is often found in the people, and that beauty is not tarnished by the often ugly rancor of national elections.

People of the Great Plains are drawn together by collective needs and, as a result of their coming together, communities are sustained. Political pundits are far too quick to conclude that places like Kansas and other Great Plains states are solidly "Republican red." In that red scheme, individualism is stressed to the point of eliminating the collective action of individuals. Yet collective action is what sustains Great Plains communities. While the partisan red/blue structure might be apt to explain electoral outcomes, it does not explain community politics. Community builders are still going strong in Kansas and elsewhere throughout the Great Plains. The diversity of such individuals is fascinating, as is the common spirit through which they work together to make community life viable.

CHAPTER 4

George McGovern

Serving the Plains and Beyond

Good politics on the Great Plains is usually derived from individuals knowing each other, acting together for the common good, and enriching community life. Individual autonomy is respected; however, individuals seek out members of the larger community in order to make life worth living. Knowing beyond one's self drives good political activity throughout the state of South Dakota. South Dakotans, much like people in other Great Plains jurisdictions, are community seekers. George McGovern represents the community of spirit shared by so many South Dakotans—past and present.

My mother was born in Aberdeen, South Dakota, and graduated from Mobridge High School. She was an astute observer of government and implementer of good politics, as evidenced by raising nine kids and never once raising her voice. Her Great Plains roots led her to stress that an individual is in charge of his or her own happiness and that, if able, you must contribute to the greater good. She required that we smile and get to know everyone we meet. I was raised, or rather schooled, in this demand to reach out and know my community. From my mom I often became a beneficiary of this South Dakota style. While attending Creighton University I had several South Dakota friends whom I would bring home from time to time. Over a carefully prepared feast my mom would turn her attention to getting to know my friends. She was always able to connect each friend with a fellow South Dakotan. The community connections were comforting.

South Dakotans (and North Dakotans as well) can be considered community seekers, as they are always willing to take part in the life of the population around them. South Dakotans seem to always know everyone within the state's borders and maybe even a few people from North Dakota. A spirit of cooperative plains politics brought North and South Dakota together through their Humanities Councils, for example. The two jurisdictions celebrated their 125th anniversaries with the program "Two States One Book," as reported by Lauren Donovan in the *Bismarck Tribune*.

The 2014 event pulled in Kathleen Norris, a longtime resident of Lemon, South Dakota, and author of the *New York Times* best seller *Dakota: A Spiritual Geography*, to discuss her work. During this event Norris offered that "people here are more sane, and I think that's going to help. The values are pretty deep, and the people coming here have good values too; they're here because they want to support their family." This is a familiar observation, echoing Richard Edwards's description of Old Stanley and continuing to the present. This wanting to know each other truly can build better politics and community, and from this "knowing" characteristic emerge thoughtful leaders. South Dakotans do not look away from others but rather look to serve others and pull them into the larger community.

The popular South Dakota slogan "Great Faces, Great Places"—beyond the obvious reference to Mount Rushmore's George Washington, Thomas Jefferson, Abraham Lincoln, and Theodore Roosevelt—suggests that this plains state forms a connection between great people and great places to live. There are many reasons why appreciation of place or community life seems so boundless in South Dakota and in other Great Plains

5. George McGovern, U.S. senator and contributor to life on the Great Plains. Library of Congress, Prints and Photographs Division, *U.S. News & World Report* Magazine Collection, LC-DIG-ppmsca-19602.

states. Political leaders discussed earlier made a positive difference in their communities, and South Dakota is no exception. George McGovern easily merits inclusion in this group.

South Dakotans' capacious and endearing ability to seem to know nearly every person in the state gives clues to the type of residents and leaders who have emerged from its towns and cities. McGovern, like his fellow South Dakotans, seemed to be genetically marked with this community trait—as if it was part of the South Dakota genome and further nurtured by caring individuals. The nurturing of community values over time was a foundational force in his public life.

McGovern was born in Avon, South Dakota, in 1922. The community of Avon provided a stable place for McGovern and his family, proclaiming itself a "small town with a big heart." The community remains vital despite its population of only five hundred, a size typical of many communities of the Great

Plains. The Methodist church, over which McGovern's father presided, now serves as a museum for the community. Although his stay there was short, Avon proudly claims McGovern among its famous residents. When he was three years old, McGovern and his family moved to Canada, but they eventually traveled back to South Dakota, where they made Mitchell home for the rest of McGovern's youth. Mitchell provided many opportunities for McGovern to develop political and community skills.

Just as it is today, Mitchell was a vibrant community during McGovern's school days. The Corn Palace, built in 1921, offers an interesting architectural dedication to area farmers. The building draws thousands of visitors each year and symbolizes the value of king corn. McGovern was shaped by the region's agriculture and its way of life.

As a high school student, McGovern honed his academic and social skills at Mitchell High School, graduating in 1940. He excelled on the debate team—an experience that would serve him well throughout his years of public service. There was no luxury of anonymity, as everyone seemingly knew each other, including others' individual strengths and weaknesses. The easy connection between school and social life served as a conduit to greater community involvement, which was reinforced by his home life as well. Social capital is derived from a variety of community-building sources, and as Robert Putnam reminds us, religion is often a primary source.

The McGovern household fostered a community orientation, driven by the Methodist social gospel, which was outward looking and directed followers to care for their community. The Methodism of McGovern's father, coupled with the communitarian elements of the Great Plains, provided a solid foundation for McGovern's politics, which were firmly based in social justice theology and practice, reinforced by family and community. His theoretical groundings drove his political practice, and the coupling of theory and practice served him well in the political world. While the influence of his father was imprinted early, McGovern's virtues and the execution of governing principles were up to him. McGovern also drew on the extensive social networks and social capital of his home communities. His experiences in Avon and Mitchell provided a launching point for his leadership as well as his political skills and will.

The Call to Serve

Communities in the Great Plains were greatly impacted by the Great Depression, which locally included severe drought and the dust bowl, as well as World War II and its lingering effects. McGovern was as affected by these hard times as were his fellow South Dakotans and all residents of the Great Plains. South Dakota's small population and tightly connected communities responded to the hard times by sharing, and the community-minded responses no doubt were catalysts that drew many people, in addition to McGovern, into political service.

McGovern found his commitment to serve others both in his religion and in this community culture of sharing, which appealed to him. He saw that whether living in Avon, Mitchell, or Aberdeen, and whether one's faith was Methodist, Catholic, or none, helping one's neighbor was a path to a meaningful and full life, a perspective shared by many other South Dakotans.

Just a forty-eight-mile jog down Highway 50 from Avon was Geddes, the home of another great community contributor and Democrat, James J. Exon. Exon, born a year earlier than McGovern, in 1921, later moved south to Nebraska, where he served as governor and U.S. senator as well as holding three other elected offices; he was another leader born into the culture of giving back. Farther north, in Aberdeen, South Dakota, lived other McGoverns, Fred and Magdalene and Walter and Marie. Walter and Fred were brothers, and Magdalene and Marie were sisters. Their marriages were enhanced by their shared political concerns. (I know this firsthand—Walter and Marie were my grandparents, and Fred and Magdalene were my great-uncle and great-aunt.) They had no genetic relationship to George and were Catholics rather than Methodists, but like George, they were community-minded Democrats driven by the teachings of social justice. Fred was the sheriff of Aberdeen, and his wife, Magdalene, was one of the first female pharmacists to graduate from the University of Minnesota. Walter and Marie were activists in the Democratic Party, and Walter often took on leadership roles at the local level. From time to time their paths would cross with George. Being part of community, sharing in the Dakota culture of knowing everyone, and acting on the obligation to serve were some of the shared traits (although not genetic).

During his youth, George McGovern witnessed daunting natural and economic hardships, ranging from severe natural droughts to the Great Depression. He learned that collective responses by civic-minded individuals can bring about a better life, and he saw that somehow his neighbors and friends persevered through austere and generous living. During hard times families shared meals with those in dire need; sometimes they left food out on the front porch or backyard picnic table so that a hungry stranger could obtain a home-cooked meal without any questions. McGovern was shaped by such experiences and embraced this caring milieu, so that his political understanding became centered on outward service.

He also found that religion—both belief and practice—influenced his political outlook. Bishop Deborah Lieder Kiesey remarked of McGovern, "Faith and action were very closely related to him. A man of really deep faith, his passion and energy has caused worldwide good. His work to end world hunger speaks volumes." McGovern's political philosophy was heavily influenced by the social messages of his Methodist foundation, and in many ways his political identity was an extension of his faith. In his 2011 book, *What It Means to Be a Democrat*, McGovern wrote that he followed a path set by John Wesley, "who believed that it was our responsibility to show compassion for the homeless, the sick, the vulnerable; for miners and factory workers. From my earliest days, that message—which, at its center, is about basic human compassion—took root deep in my soul." The cynical observer of politics might argue that such an idealistic outlook would be disastrous for modern government, but for McGovern it provided a lifelong source of hope and energy.

The young McGovern considered going into the ministry. This was a tried and true route in his family: making a positive impact through a congregation. The church provided an organizational basis to build community and strengthen positive social relationships. Aware of this potential, McGovern enrolled in and graduated from Dakota Wesleyan University in Mitchell. He served as a bomber pilot over Europe in World War II, and when he returned he headed to Northwestern University to earn his PhD in American history.

After graduating, McGovern returned to teach at his alma mater, Dakota Wesleyan. To draw upon his familiar roots seemed like a perfect way to employ his talents. Professor McGovern was a masterful young teacher who had a special talent for empowering others. One former student, Dorothy Schwieder, who grew up in a small town west of the Missouri River in South Dakota, wrote that "McGovern's courses made world events and politics understandable for the first time, and they conveyed the possibility of betterment and change." Upon entering in 1951, her small class of 150 (at most) primarily came from small towns and rural areas throughout South Dakota. "While our transition to college was exciting," Schwieder said, "it was also circumscribed." It was a move from small towns to a small college on "familiar ground," so "while Wesleyan offered the rich promise of higher education, it also remained a product of its place and time."

For anyone fortunate enough to experience college then, education was empowering. And when a college graduate remained in the region, his or her community was enriched. But there has long been a cycle of education followed by departure from the Great Plains, which has deprived those communities of their brightest youth. If a college graduate finds little economic opportunity at home, then he or she tends to leave the area. McGovern's goal with his students was to empower them to make their communities better, but he understood the limits of what he could accomplish in the classroom. Searching for other career opportunities, he left Dakota Wesleyan to embark on a more formal political path, primarily in electoral politics.

Electoral Politics: Serving from the National and Local Levels

Electoral politics still provides the democratic construct for a better life, despite the cynical claims so fashionable among pundits. McGovern enthusiastically stepped up to run for electoral office several times during his political career. He had developed a strong understanding of community service, and since his debate days in high school and college, he thrived as an advocate. It seemed only natural for him to run for political office. He was often successful, but he also suffered his fair share of defeats. He is often remembered for his failed run for president; indeed, it consumes most of the attention of pundits. But his community contributions can only be partially understood by his electoral adventures or misadventures.

In 1957 McGovern was elected to serve in the U.S. House of Representatives. The House allowed him to translate his understanding of theory and religion into the practice of politics.

McGovern found ample opportunity to draw upon his family roots, South Dakota culture, and overall concern with linking agricultural life to his broader goals. In the House he found an outlet in which to use his understanding of the political process to serve South Dakotans and many others. In 1960 he ran for the U.S. Senate but lost. His defeat, however, did not remove him from the national stage, because President John F. Kennedy appointed him to serve as the director of Food for Peace, a program of the U.S. Agency for International Development. McGovern was well suited for this position, which allowed him to showcase his ability to link hunger issues to South Dakota agriculture. McGovern had long been concerned about reducing hunger, and he found that the formulation and execution of food programs fit very well with the social gospel of his upbringing *and* with serving the farmers' interests back home. The work coupled McGovern's call for social justice with the practical need of pleasing Great Plains farmers.

While in the U.S. House of Representatives and later as the director of Food for Peace, McGovern pushed to utilize agricultural surpluses to benefit his home base and feed the world. At the time, farmers received no economic benefit from their surplus crops. Sandy Ross, a global food policy expert from Australia, explains in a 2007 article that "food aid was used initially as a bilateral (and rather blunt) instrument to get rid of surpluses." In the late 1950s, McGovern and Hubert Humphrey led Congress in a domestic debate that resulted in renaming the food aid program the Food for Peace Program. During the 1960 presidential race, both Richard Nixon and John F. Kennedy pledged to work for "a multilateral food program," in which "multilateral and bilateral food aids" would no longer be seen as mutually exclusive. In other words, the bilateral agreements between nations were bolstered with multilateral agreements that went further by extending food to providing agencies.

McGovern's experience in the House and as director of Food for Peace drew on his pragmatic, problem-solving side—he was able to serve his constituents in a manner that fit his character as well as theirs. After all, Great Plains farmers, whether in South Dakota or Texas, take comfort knowing their work feeds communities. McGovern both served his South Dakota constituents and crafted programs that allowed his constituents opportunities to mitigate worldwide hunger.

The political dynamic involving hunger and food has almost always been of interest to farmers of the Great Plains. McGovern, like Virginia Smith and other officials of the Great Plains, believed crop surpluses and hungry people should not coexist. Farmers were often able to produce surplus crops. Unfortunately, mechanisms to deliver surplus food to those in greatest need frequently failed or were inadequate. When his staff at the Office for Food for Peace complained about farm surpluses in 1961, McGovern told them that "there was no such thing as 'a burdensome farm surplus' as long as there were hungry children in the world." Rather, he said, "Let's praise our farmers for their skill, hard work, and productivity and tell them that they make it possible for us to have the great privilege of feeding our fellow humans." McGovern's leadership reinforced the value of his South Dakota community while attacking world hunger. He had found a leadership post that drew on his core beliefs and resulted in policies that linked his community base to the larger world.

McGovern was elected to the U.S. Senate in 1962 and reelected in 1968 and 1974. As a senator, he continued to push his interest in alleviating hunger while serving the South Dakota community. Gerald Oppenheimer and Daniel Benrubi wrote in the *American Journal of Public Health* that Senator McGovern was viewed as a friend of the agriculture industry in his role as chair of the Select Committee on Nutrition and

Human Needs, also known as the "McGovern Committee" (1968–77). Some even regarded his politics as serving special interests at the cost of promoting healthy food habits. Many of the foods at issue, meat and more meat, were part of what McGovern and his constituents believed to be a healthy Great Plains diet. McGovern was urged to disassociate himself from agricultural interests and instead align his views with those of new "nutritional forces" that were contrary to the grain and beef production of his home state's farmers and ranchers.

McGovern was not apologetic about pushing South Dakota agricultural interests as part of his program to mitigate hunger. In fact, the pushback came from forces outside his home state. Many health advocates claimed that the cattle industry was producing an unhealthy diet and that grain production related to the cattle industry was harmful to local and worldwide populations. The South Dakota interests that McGovern championed seemed in conflict with emerging health standards. The political battle picked up steam in 1973 as McGovern's Senate committee debated new nutritional standards. Marshal Matz, general counsel for the committee, argued that McGovern should be the broker for the new standards and that medical evidence against the meat industry should not be discounted. McGovern rejected such counsel and in a prepared statement observed that there was not a link between meat consumption and disease; rather, he argued that beef is "an excellent source of protein."

McGovern's stance in the beef controversy showed his commitment to the communities of his state and other residents of the Great Plains. Many South Dakotans made a living in beef and related grain production. But McGovern also intended to utilize South Dakota agricultural products to feed masses beyond the state's borders. He believed it was obvious that smart policy could provide the world with surplus crops harvested from South Dakota and Great Plains fields, so he championed both his constituents and the food they produced; he was glad to deliver economic and community-sustaining benefits.

McGovern and Kansas Senator Bob Dole

After leaving the Senate, McGovern was appointed U.S. ambassador to the UN Food and Agriculture Organization (1998–2001), and in 2001 he was appointed to be the goodwill ambassador on world hunger. His drive to mitigate hunger was shared by his longtime friend and colleague Senator Bob Dole (Republican from Kansas, 1969–96; see chapter 5). Since the 1970s and through their post-Senate days, the two men had pushed for the expansion of the U.S. school lunch program around the globe. They cooperated in lobbying for the Farm Bill of 2002, which included provisions to utilize food gathered from the Great Plains to feed and empower the world's neediest populations. As Chuck Raasch explained in 2012 in *USA Today*, "The story of how these two Dust Bowl boys came together in the twilight of their lives to fight hunger has been largely drowned out in the age of extreme partisanship. Dole and McGovern late in life discovered a common ground that had often eluded them across the partisan aisle in the United States Senate."

Two Great Plains statesmen, Dole and McGovern, crossed partisan boundaries and stayed united by their shared understanding of place, leading to the legislation bearing their names, the George McGovern–Robert Dole International Food for Education and Child Nutrition Act. According to the Foreign Agricultural Service, the act "helps support education, child development and food security in low-income, food-deficit countries around the globe." More than 30 million people are currently served. The program established under the act operates on a dual premise: one, that boxes of food marked with "USA" create lifetime impressions of mercy for the young, vulnerable, and hungry; and two, that sopping up U.S. agricultural surpluses in the name of diplomacy helps farmers in wheat, corn, and cattle country. It provides U.S. agricultural commodities and financial and technical assistance "to support school feeding and maternal and child nutrition projects." The program is intended to empower schoolchildren and support maternal health so that coming generations can markedly improve their lives. McGovern was again able to extrapolate lessons from his South Dakota understanding of community in order to provide benefits on a world scale.

Perseverance in the Face of Hardship

McGovern would have been the first to acknowledge his frailties. This work on Great Plains politics is not aimed at raising McGovern or any other figure to the status of some sort of flawless superhero. McGovern persevered through various failures and setbacks. For example, he fathered a child before marriage with a woman other than his first and only wife. The FBI, which followed his work and movements, hoped to discover other transgressions but failed. He led an upstanding life, and any frailties did not deter his steadfast commitment to others. His personal peccadillos, however interesting to critics, are not relevant to how McGovern championed the cause of his community.

McGovern's political defeats—in his initial run for the Senate in 1960, in his devastating loss to Richard Nixon in the 1972 presidential election, and in his final try for Senate reelection in 1980—further serve as a reminder that service to others requires a certain level of perseverance. McGovern's losses failed to deter him from public life, especially in formal efforts to mitigate world hunger. Perseverance was indeed a gift he possessed and is a trait commonly held by community builders.

These setbacks as well as McGovern's successes were greatly tempered by the life and death of his daughter Terry McGovern, the third of his five children. Alcohol and depression raged through Terry's life until she died at the age of forty-six. She froze to death in Madison, Wisconsin, and was found with a blood alcohol content well beyond the legal limit. As one would suspect, George was deeply saddened by the tragic event; the "what ifs" percolated within him. Public life and personal life intertwine. Leadership has hidden costs, for McGovern as it did for Wilma Mankiller.

During his twilight years, George McGovern's interest in feeding those in need and championing peaceful politics did not wane. The Mitchell newspaper, the *Daily Republic*, reported that McGovern urged President Obama to address hunger and food issues as well as underscoring the need to remove U.S. troops from Afghanistan. In an opinion piece directed at the new president, the Mitchell paper reported, "McGovern plugged the George McGovern–Robert Dole International Food for Education and Child Nutrition Act, which he said is underfunded but is delivering school lunches to millions of children. He said such programs encourage children to attend school and grow into better citizens. 'It would cost a small fraction of warfare's cost,' McGovern wrote in closing, 'but it might well be a stronger antidote to terrorism. There will always be time for another war. But hunger can't wait.'"

Because of his keen and persistent interest in linking political service to the community, McGovern continued to include food and reducing hunger in his political agenda until the day he died. In the autumn of each year, he executed his political will by providing food for his South Dakota community. In 2011 South Dakota Democrats established George McGovern Day not only to honor McGovern and raise party funds but also to urge communities to feed the hungry. Feeding South Dakota was launched, and McGovern characterized the organization: "In times of pressing need—whether your family has been displaced by flooding or your paycheck isn't covering the rising cost of food—Feeding South Dakota is our state's first responder in the fight against hunger."

McGovern experienced electoral successes and failures, but his orientation to serve others is what defined him as a positive force in the political world. This was prominently demonstrated by his efforts to help farmers throughout South Dakota feed those in need. George McGovern's brand of politics was not driven by selfish partisan politics but rather embedded in and imbued with care for others.

CHAPTER 5

Bob Dole

The Man from Russell

Robert J. "Bob" Dole, the long-serving U.S. congressman and senator from Kansas, was born on July 22, 1923, in Russell, Kansas. At the time Russell, in north central Kansas, was, like many settlements in the region, struggling to survive the harsh environment of the plains. The town's population was 1,700 in 1920, peaked at 6,483 in 1950, and lost nearly a third of its people by 2015, dropping to 4,534. Declining populations put great stress on towns, and the remaining residents face the challenge of maintaining their communities, a test that can elicit an ethic of community-centered action. Bob Dole witnessed firsthand this culture of community regression and the need for shared action by townsfolk to overcome it. He learned both his personal habits and his political orientation from his parents and the wider Russell community. His parents were hard working and civic minded, his dad doing a variety of jobs, such as selling eggs and produce and running a creamery, and his mother working as a skilled sewing machine salesperson. At an early age he came to understand the value of cooperation and hard work. When not at school Dole often assisted his dad as needed, also working as a soda jerk at the local drugstore soda fountain. These early experiences allowed him to develop social skills and his jocular, sometimes caustic one-liners. The social abilities stayed with him and served him well during his long political career. He became famous for his one-liners.

Dole attended Russell High School, where he was a good student and an outstanding athlete. His athletic skills were well known throughout Kansas. He thoroughly enjoyed the individual demands of sports and liked as well the interplay with his teammates. He was recruited by the famed Coach Phogg Allen to play basketball at the University of Kansas (KU), where he also signed up to play football and run track. He entered KU in 1941.

At the University

At Kansas, Dole showed he could balance a variety of demands: academics, work, athletics, and quite extensive social commitments. His letters (housed at the KU archives) show growing appreciation for social life. Campus activities impressed Dole, and he was eager to be part of them. During his freshman year, KU beat its rival Kansas State University in football, and the students decided to take the following Monday off from classes. Dole wrote his parents, "Did you read about the K.U. students taking a day off without the Chancellor's permission? Around 3000 students paraded to the Chancellor's house asking him to dismiss Monday classes; when he refused the students refused to go to their classes and spent all day celebrating the K-State victory."

Another letter home, undated, suggests the capacious social aspect of Dole's college life. He wrote, "We have a party next weekend so I won't be able to come home. It's called the Red Day Inn. Everybody comes dressed like a cowboy or cowgirl which considering I have no costume, I'm faced with a problem." He asked his mom to send him the appropriate party attire. Dole loved his college friends and they in turn loved him; he seemed to be a natural in social settings. His inclination for the social aspects of campus life served as a teaser for his later interest in politics. Dole's letters home reveal other aspects of his community life. He was interested in his schoolwork, his fraternity, Kappa Sigma, sports, family, church, food, and much more. Being able to balance so many activities with such apparent ease made him an interesting student. His social skills, including always holding an outward gaze and focusing on others rather than himself, as many young men his age did, would serve him well.

In 1942 Dole joined the U.S. Army Reserves, and his life was forever changed by his World War II service. He went through basic training and became a combat infantry officer. In 1944 he was shipped out to Europe, initially serving near Rome in a relatively safe area, but in 1945 he was transferred to Italy's Po Valley, a lethal region still infested with tough German troops. Despite Dole's relative inexperience in combat, he was ordered to lead an assault against a German machine-gun nest. The day of the assault was, as Dole put it, "the day that changed my life." He was hit by machine-gun fire and gravely wounded. As noted in an online biography, Dole suffered a "shattered right shoulder, fractured vertebrae in his neck and spine, paralysis from the neck down, metal shrapnel throughout his body and a damaged kidney." These wounds, life-endangering and highly debilitating, consigned Dole to a long, difficult, and painful rehabilitation process and a lifetime of disability.

Dole was hospitalized for thirty-nine months, during which he suffered several life-threatening infections and underwent numerous painful surgeries. The rehabilitation process offered Dole insights into the benefits of good governmental assistance. His prolonged rehabilitation stay opened Dole's eyes to disabled soldiers and the positive role government could play in providing benefits and care for these citizens. Although he would later be an icon for conservative Republicans, the dreadful aspects of war sensitized him and heightened his care for humanity, a

6. Robert J. "Bob" Dole, recovering from wounds suffered during World War II. Courtesy of the Robert and Elizabeth Dole Archive and Special Collections, University of Kansas.

perspective whose foundation had been laid on the plains of Kansas. His closeness to his family and his fondness for Russell and KU enriched his understanding of community. Despite his political inclination, Dole was not closed to the idea that individuals could greatly benefit from government.

Perhaps even Dole's notion of teamwork, shaped by his athletic past, informed his understanding of what it meant to be a Republican. After all, he was a team player and the government was a key part of the game. This perspective stuck with him, and his willingness to cross party lines and work with Democrats as he matured into his role as a Republican statesman should be of little surprise. His political actions were influenced by his social, perhaps folksy, "Great Plain-ish" understanding of community and politics, in which government was not bad.

Dole benefited from other governmental services in addition to medical care. He had entered KU interested in being a physician, but he abandoned that ambition because of his severe war injuries. Still, he lost none of his interest in serving others. So he shifted his focus to law and utilized the GI Bill to continue his education, first at the University of Arizona and then Washburn University. In 1952 Dole received his undergraduate and law degrees from Washburn University, but already in 1950, while still in school, Dole had won a seat in the Kansas House of Representatives. He served one two-year term and used the legislative experience to build his political capital.

In 1952 Dole ran to be the Russell County attorney and won. Serving for eight years, he was adept in his ability to navigate a diverse collection of legal issues, from agriculture to petroleum, using the social-networking skills he developed in his youth. His legal skills were solid, and he gained an additional layer of experience serving his home community. As the Russell County attorney, he took on a variety of local issues and succeeded, for example, in ridding farmers of the severance tax associated with oil and gas found on agricultural land. Dole was good at serving his community, and his interest in community building pushed him toward greater political possibilities. He was ready to serve on a larger scale.

Dole found his opportunity in 1960 when seven-term congressman Wint Smith chose not to seek reelection in Kansas's Sixth District. Dole faced a competitive situation as he launched his campaign. Melissa Brunkan, in a 2014 article in the journal *Popular Music and Society* quotes Dole speaking about his concerns: "At the beginning of the campaign I faced a special problem of name identification. It wasn't only that Keith Sebelius was already a familiar figure throughout the district and I was not. What really complicated things was a third candidate on the ballot, a state senator named Phillip J. Doyle. I was less worried about Doyle's appeal to the farm vote than about the confusion that was sure to arise from the similarity of our names."

Dole's competitive nature and ingenuity served him well against this roster of credible candidates. His campaign developed a quirky, musical overtone, especially after he enlisted the help of four college-aged, musically talented women, the Bob-o-links. The quartet consisted of Dorothy and Delores Voss, Nancy Humes, and Bonnie Naegele Langdon. The Bob-o-links appeared at events throughout the sprawling district, singing original Dole-centered verses to the melodies of popular songs and distributing Dole songbooks. They solved the name-recognition problem at a time when television advertising was of little use in western Kansas, since there were few television stations or home television sets. Dole's novel campaigning paid off, and in 1960 he made his way to the U.S. House of Representatives.

Dole the Trustee

Once elected, a legislator can see his or her job of representing constituents in either of two ways. The legislator can act as the constituents' delegate, checking public opinion polls and voting according to what the majority dictates, or the legislator can act as a trustee, taking in knowledge gained from the office and acting in what he or she sees as the best interest of the greater community. Dole as a legislator usually acted as a trustee. Although he never lost sight of his Great Plains roots, he advocated for what he thought would be best for the greater good, occasionally putting him at odds with his constituents. The best example is civil rights.

Dole supported both the Civil Rights Act of 1964 and the Voting Rights Act of 1965. Kansas was the site of the 1954 landmark desegregation case *Brown v. Board of Education of Topeka*. Among Kansans, full citizenship rights for black people was highly controversial. But Dole acted on the basis of his understanding of the greater good of the community: He knew that in order to bring about a better community life for Kansans, discrimination based on race or any immutable characteristic should not be tolerated. And so he joined 135 other Republican House members and twenty-seven Republican senators in voting for the historic legislation. Later, as a U.S. senator, Dole would remain a consistent supporter of civil rights, sponsoring an impressive list of civil rights legislation. Beginning in 1970 he supported creating a national holiday to honor Martin Luther King Jr., and in the Ninety-Eighth Congress (1983–84) he was one of the thirty-four cosponsors for the bill that finally created MLK Day. In 1982 Dole voted to extend and expand the Voting Rights Act. He likewise supported legislation empowering women.

In 1968 Dole won the nomination to replace retiring Republican senator Frank Carlson. He easily defeated both the Democratic and Prohibition Party candidates and began a long career in the Senate. He was reelected in 1974, 1980, 1986, and 1992, finally resigning from the Senate in 1996 when he became the Republican Party's nominee for president. He served as leader of the Senate Republicans from 1985 to 1996, twice being majority leader.

While Dole could be a fierce Republican partisan—from 1971 to 1973, as chairman of the Republican National Committee, he was the party's chief evangelist—his career in both the House and Senate was marked by a conspicuous willingness to work with Democrats. For example, the personal perspective gained from his war injuries and residual disabilities seemed to make him a natural champion for citizens with disabilities. In 1969 he lectured President Richard Nixon on the need to provide legislation for disabled Americans:

> It is a group who no one joins by personal choice—a group whose requirements for membership are not based on age, sex, wealth, education, skin color, religious beliefs, political party, power or prestige. As a minority, it has always known exclusion; maybe not exclusion from the front of the bus, but perhaps from even climbing aboard it; maybe not exclusion from pursuing advanced education, but perhaps from experiencing any formal education; maybe not exclusion from day-to-day life itself, but perhaps from an adequate opportunity to develop and contribute to his or her fullest capacity. It is a minority, yet a group to which at least one out of every five Americans belongs. Mr. President, I speak today about 42 million citizens of our Nation who are physically, mentally or emotionally handicapped.

He strongly advocated for the Americans with Disabilities Act (ADA), which with his leadership was passed on July 26, 1990.

Dole was long inclusive in his worldview and a team player and social being. He reminded his constituents that Kansas was about building community, not tearing it down. As a trustee, he was often willing to reach across the partisan divide, something unusual today. One of his greatest accomplishments was his work in 1983 to preserve Social Security. The system was in serious financial peril, and Dole worked energetically with Republicans and Democrats to fashion a solution. Senator Patrick Moynihan, a New York Democrat, noted that Dole always liked to talk in interviews or speeches about the first two weeks of 1983, when "quite literally, the Social Security system was saved. The only part of the tale he leaves out is his own role," Moynihan said. "It could not have happened without him. To the contrary, he made it happen. I was there. I so attest."

The Social Security collaboration provides insight into Dole's dedication to governing and his understanding of the importance of relationships. He knew that governing required cooperation, not selfish or quarrelsome partisanship. Years after the Social Security bailout, in 1998, Dole wrote in the *Harvard Journal on Legislation* of his proudest achievement:

> Ultimately, workable legislation required concessions from all of the parties who had a stake in the Social Security issue. While not everyone was happy with every specific recommendation, the important fact is that consensus was reached on how to save the system. My point is not that the lowest common denominator is what should pass as policy. Rather, policy, good or bad, is what will gain approval of a majority, and what the President will ultimately sign. In fact, most political scientists who study Congress would probably say that this is the real definition of policy. Our leadership must understand the importance of compromise in addition to principle, and must recognize when an opportunity for compromise exists that will serve our values and priorities more effectively than no action at all.

Dole's effort to save Social Security was, of course, service to the entire nation as much as Kansans. In his own region, Dole provided relentless support for Great Plains farmers. Here he embraced the idea, also supported by his old friend George McGovern, a Democrat, that the farmers of the Great Plains could be the driving force to alleviate domestic and world hunger. McGovern served in the Senate from 1963 to 1981, and Dole served from 1969 to 1996. They shared the painful experience of failed runs for the presidency, McGovern in 1972 and Dole in 1996. From time to time they produced loud partisan discourse, but they were drawn together by their shared interest in using food from the Great Plains and beyond to feed the hungry.

Dole battled his own party and President Reagan over the 1985 Farm Bill. The bill was encouraging to a suffering farm sector on the Great Plains, and Dole, as Senate majority leader, provided active leadership for its passage. Despite the Reagan administration's opposition and only after eleven long months of hard politicking, Dole was able to get the bill passed and signed into law by Reagan on December 23, 1985. Dole claimed the bill provided the "essential first steps in restoring hope and confidence in rural America."

Dole, like McGovern, would maintain his interest in and advocacy for the farmer during his elected years and well after. He cooperated with McGovern in lobbying for the Farm Bill of 2002, which included provisions that utilized food gathered from the Great Plains to feed and empower the world's neediest populations. Their unifying vision overrode partisan passions, and later, in 2013, the two ex-senators received a special commendation from the World Food Program, which proclaimed,

It is no exaggeration to say that every major U.S. program designed to help feed poor children bears the imprint of these two men. They helped reform the federal Food Stamp Program, known today as the Supplemental Nutrition Assistance Program or SNAP. Food stamps provide a nutritional safety net for 47 million Americans, nearly half of whom are children. Senators McGovern and Dole worked together to expand the National School Lunch Program, which today feeds more than 31 million children in schools and child care centers. And they helped to establish the Special Supplemental Food Program for Women, Infants, and Children (WIC), which provides healthy food, nutritional information, and health care referrals to nearly 9 million low-income pregnant women, mothers, and young children who are at nutrition risk.

Dole, like McGovern, was committed to utilizing the breadbasket of the Great Plains for hunger relief, and the two men refused to let partisan differences stop them from promoting policies rooted in their Great Plains base. In 2006 *USA Today* reported on their ongoing efforts: "Thirty years after the national school lunch program made its debut, hunger relief organizations and food service providers are pushing to raise awareness about a virtually unknown federal service for children: free breakfast." The paper quoted Dole as musing about his partnership with McGovern, "We've been odd for a long time. In the Senate, even though we disagreed on other issues, we had a lot of common ground." Together, Dole and McGovern knew how to put partisan politics aside to govern for the children and the hungry at home and abroad. Their Great Plains roots deeply shaped how they approached food policy, and their shared commitment to do what is right for the larger community tempered their partisan differences.

Home and Away

Dole loved his home, Russell, Kansas, and always kept in view the importance of preserving that which is good on the plains. Even though he was often referred to as "Beltway Bob" because of his long tenure and deep connections in the Washington establishment, he remained oriented to and in touch with his home community. On June 13, 2012, as his eighty-eighth birthday approached, he traveled to Russell, where he was met by residents who were, by all accounts, delighted to see him return. In turn, Dole displayed love for his birthplace. "It's still home," he said. "There's only one home, and that's wherever you grew up."

Dole, the go-to guy in sports, the reliable worker, and the key social player for college parties, matured into a leader whose political offices allowed him to reach out and serve the greater good. Yes, Dole was from a red state, but he was also much more than simply another Republican from a Republican state—he deeply maintained his commitment to serving others and preserving community, much in line with other Great Plains leaders.

CHAPTER 6

Elizabeth Byrd

A Legacy in the Face of Discrimination

The view from the fringes of the Great Plains reveals the region's sweeping entirety. Location not only reinforces identity but also offers a glimpse of other geographic and cultural attachments. Wyoming is one such fringe location, with mountain ranges to the west and a sizeable land mass and population on the eastern edge that clearly belongs to the Great Plains. These edge places offer their residents multiple opportunities for community building. Wyoming has been host to a variety of political leaders, ranging from Nellie Tayloe Ross (first woman governor in the nation) to Richard "Dick" Cheney, secretary of defense and vice president under George W. Bush. It also was home to the Black 14, University of Wyoming (UW) African American football players who, in the fall of 1969, prominently protested against the racial policies of Brigham Young University, such as the barring of African Americans from church leadership. The UW coach, Lloyd Elliot, had a rule against public protest. For their actions, these politically active players were dismissed by the coach and their politics snuffed. It should be noted that the University of Wyoming administration supported the coach.

Taking part in the political process, although so very important, certainly was and is difficult, even for a skilled politician. Such was the case for Harriet Elizabeth "Liz" Byrd.

Byrd was a highly successful Wyoming political contributor and community builder, but her contributions have often been overlooked. An African American, Byrd grew up in one of the few African American households in the state, and while she encountered racism early in her life, she learned not to let it limit her ability to move forward. Byrd demonstrated a new dimension of how good politics builds good community life. Building community requires attention to discrimination because discrimination ultimately destroys a sense of community. Byrd was subjected to racial intolerance, but she simply decided that she would not let discrimination keep her from achieving her goals in life.

Byrd was a fourth-generation Wyomingite. Her great-grandparents brought her paternal grandfather, Charles J. Rhone, to Wyoming as a child in 1876. Rhone was a prominent cowboy who later worked as a railroader. Her parents, Buck and Sadie Rhone, found success in Wyoming. Buck was an accomplished mechanic for Union Pacific, and a park on Central Avenue in Cheyenne was named after him. Liz was born in 1926, raised in Cheyenne, and attended Cheyenne schools. She graduated from Cheyenne Central High School in 1943. She enjoyed the sense of community as well as the educational opportunities offered by school and the family's social networks. Her upbringing in Cheyenne, despite its casual racism, centered on her nurturing family and varied community offerings. Her academic success placed her in a position to move on to college, and with her love of education, she decided to be a teacher. She set her sights on attending the University of Wyoming, then and still the only state university in Wyoming, believing that traveling the fifty miles to Laramie seemed perfect.

Byrd was shocked and disappointed when the university informed her that she had been denied admission because of

7. Harriet Elizabeth "Liz" Byrd, shown teaching students in Cheyenne, Wyoming, governed well in the classroom and beyond. Harriett Elizabeth Byrd Family Papers, box 3, folder 6, American Heritage Center, University of Wyoming.

her race. The rejection was confusing for her because she loved the university and had experienced a childhood in which race issues, while always present, were never this stark. She felt the harm of the decision keenly. But, refusing to be defeated, Byrd reluctantly left Wyoming to seek a college that would accept her. She attended West Virginia State University, a historically black university, and graduated in 1949.

Byrd sought a job teaching elementary students in her hometown public schools. But as Rodger McDaniel reported in his July 4, 2015, column for the *Wyoming Tribune-Eagle*, the Cheyenne schools initially decided not to hire Byrd because they feared white parents would not want her to educate and discipline their children. Denied again, she found employment as a civilian instructor at Warren Air Force Base in Cheyenne. Finally, in 1959, the Laramie County School District reversed its earlier decision, and Byrd's persistence paid off when she was hired as an elementary schoolteacher. She taught for twenty-seven years.

In 1947 she married James Byrd, who was also a racial pioneer. In 1966 he was appointed Cheyenne's chief of police, the first African American within the state to hold that position. In 1975 Governor Ed Herschler appointed him director of the Wyoming Office of Highway Safety, and in 1977 President Jimmy Carter named him a U.S. marshal for the state of Wyoming. Together, Liz and James, both personal successes, had tremendous impacts on the Cheyenne community.

Although originally denied entrance to the school, Byrd persisted in wanting to attend the University of Wyoming. She applied again, this time for graduate school, and was admitted. She graduated in 1976 with an MA degree.

In 1980 Liz Byrd decided to run for elective office, and when she won she became the first African American female state legislator in Wyoming history. (William Jefferson Hardin was the first African American legislator, serving in 1879 in Wyoming Territory.) She served in the Wyoming House from 1980 to 1988 and in the Wyoming Senate from 1988 to 1992. Byrd made many types of contributions to her students, neighbors, community, and state as a teacher, community leader, and elected official before she died in 2015.

Classroom Influence

Her archives, which can be accessed at her beloved University of Wyoming, reveal that as a teacher Byrd was "known for teaching her students about local, county, and state government and had provided legislation for her second grade class to participate in the legislative process." She provided lessons in and out of the classroom that emphasized her belief in community and the importance of being an active citizen. Additionally, her lessons delivered instruction on how to build community life.

She made a point of committing to each student in her classroom. She was socially vibrant. We can catch a glimpse of her personality in her archives. For example, she offers details of a memorable Valentine's Day. Her husband, Jim, surprised her by bringing cookies for her entire second-grade class at Deming Elementary School. She remarked that she was "just as delighted as her students." That he brought cookies for her and her students was a small signal of her—and her husband's—community orientation. Reading the papers in her archives, one quickly sees the sense of satisfaction Byrd gained by serving others. Her classroom experiences are indicative of a leadership style that built community rather than focusing on self-promotion.

Through associations she made in her teaching, Byrd began to assert herself as a community-minded leader. She took advantage of the collective social capital provided by her teaching profession and worked on important community-building projects. One such project was designed to aid newborns and mothers. In cooperation with other teachers, she raised money to create mother-baby packets. The packets contained a variety of essential items for newborns. They were intended to ensure a healthy start for the newborns and, additionally, to provide educational materials for the mothers. Byrd was committed to early childhood health and education.

Liz Byrd, like other community leaders whose lives we have explored, had a deep concern for taking care of those in need, especially the hungry. In partnership with the Salvation Army and the Federal Food Distribution Program, she worked to directly reduce hunger in her community. Her efforts seem to have had no boundaries. She knew that churches in the Great Plains provided organizational networks that connected the broader community. She was a member of St. Mary's Catholic Church, but she was catholic in her determination to serve others of alternate denominations. She sponsored the A M E Methodist Church fundraiser to build a kitchen that would ultimately serve those in need. For her, the connection between food and building community was obvious: she wanted her community to reduce hunger, and that was not to be limited by the form of church membership.

Overcoming Discrimination in the Equality State

When Byrd entered the Wyoming legislature, she sought to extend the impact she might have on her own community and, indeed, every Wyoming town. She became an advocate for her community, but that led to her becoming a champion for all who had no voice in the political process. For example, Byrd sponsored child safety-restraint legislation. According to Lori Van Pelt, writing at WyoHistory.org, Byrd's son recalled that she was especially "proud of her work on behalf of the child car-seat law 'because it saves lives.'"

Byrd was endorsed by Laramie County workers, as she was concerned with protecting everyone's jobs and believed that part-time employees should receive benefits like full-time employees as well as pay increases. Further, she believed in creating a sick-leave bank and favored self-insurance strategies that would allow money to remain in the state. She was viewed as very loyal to the people of Wyoming, who understood that her leadership was based on how to best serve fellow community members.

Byrd's most ardent campaign was as a champion of civil rights, and she was the moving force behind Wyoming's rec-ognition in 1989 of Martin Luther King Jr. Day. This push required compromise, as some argued that Wyoming already had embraced equality—its nickname is the Equality State because it was the first territory and later the first state to allow women to vote, serve on juries, and hold public office. Still, those were nineteenth-century accomplishments, and it was unclear whether the state was ready for a new commitment. Byrd's gentle but persistent leadership insisted that it was, and the path she and others found was to couple Martin Luther King Jr. Day and Wyoming Equality Day. Byrd understood that compromise was often necessary to achieve what gains were possible in the development of a diverse community life, and she prevailed.

Jesse Jackson, the famed civil rights leader, visited Cheyenne on April 20, 1989, to address a near-capacity civic center crowd and help celebrate this achievement. Byrd was sitting on stage for the big reveal, and as if referring to her work, Jackson offered this thought on how one is measured: "how you treat children in the dawn of life, how you treat poor people, how you treat old people in the sunset of life, and how you treat the stranger on the Jericho Road."

Byrd's work is not quite complete because, despite her efforts, MLK Day remains a mandatory workday for the legislative body. Her son, James Byrd, now also a fourth-term state representative, had no option but to work on MLK Day. In persevering fashion, he stated, "I would like us to adjourn on this date. It would be very nice. . . . But this is the state of Wyoming; we determine what days we want as holidays." With patience, he said, maybe at some point the majority will agree to recognize MLK Day as a day off work, but "as for now, the majority of people in the Legislature and those who make the schedule deem it as not an important day to take a holiday, and they're in charge."

Liz Byrd refused to let discrimination and prejudice prevent her from contributing to community life. She had a drive to serve others that was realized in her public and private affairs and that best characterized her understanding of place and people. She was purposeful in seeking to improve her community and her state. Sometimes people are driven out of the Great Plains by the harsh natural and physical conditions. In Byrd's case, intolerant human responses to her race could have driven her away, as discrimination in the Equality State must have been discouraging to her as well as other African Americans. The college admissions decision was but one harmful racial incident, and upon her return to Wyoming, other acts of racial hatred were visited upon her. Yet she regularly met this hostility and unfairness with the stamina not just to endure but to triumph. As a fourth-generation African American in Wyoming, she had deep resources to call upon and a collective family commitment to the community life of Wyoming.

Byrd's leadership was not without personal discomfort. At times she grew weary of racial isolation. As much as she loved Wyoming and the associated civic virtues found in many of its citizens, she expressed concerns regarding her African American heritage: "There comes a time, when day after day, you're the only black person at school, or you're the only black person at a picnic, and that gets old." But she managed to live and continue serving her community by partnering with her husband and relying on her supportive family. Like many leaders, Byrd knew how to live in harmony with her family but also knew how to socialize and have fun. The latter is important in overcoming harsh realities, especially those experienced on the Great Plains.

Byrd was a serious worker, but as her friend and fellow Cheyenne activist Rita Watson said, she knew when to be stern and when not to; work and pleasure were meshed into a personal style of leadership. Byrd was serious when she needed to be and always managed to complete the task at hand, according to Watson. The lament above reflects the real negative forces that confronted her. Byrd's notion of community was inclusive, although some in her community were not so receptive of such inclusivity. The perseverance Byrd displayed indicates that her service was for the benefit of others and not herself.

In the best sense, to borrow from Aristotle, Byrd was a political animal—an engaged citizen. Characteristics of an engaged citizen, and in turn, an effective community leader, are evidenced by the numerous connections Byrd made to others through associations. From her archives comes an astounding list of organizational involvement: Wyoming Educators Association, Laramie Senior Citizens Advisory Board, KUWR University of Wyoming Advisory Committee, United Medical Center Auxiliary, Golden K-International Kiwanis of Cheyenne, Democratic Women's Club, Retired Teachers of Cheyenne School District 1, Retired Cheyenne Altrusa, Delta Sigma Theta Sorority, Delta Kappa Gamma Society, Kappa Iota, Kappa Delta Pi, the NAACP, and the National Education Association. This lengthy list illustrates the commitment she had to being fully engaged in the greater community. These associations provided a wealth of social capital and allowed her to be an effective political and community leader.

Byrd's relationship with the University of Wyoming, the school that had crushed her first dreams of college with its rejection of her application, became a metaphor for the arc of her whole life. The university became a kind of home for Byrd, and over the years it honored her for her many contributions as an educator, citizen, and leader. Ironically, following her death, UW president Dick McGinity wrote in an email, "Liz Byrd was a true pioneer in Wyoming's educational and political history. As an educator, she displayed tremendous fortitude in overcoming racial discrimination to forge an exemplary teaching career that included a master's degree from UW in 1976." UW recognized her in 2012 as a distinguished alumna, an honor she clearly warranted. UW African American and Diaspora Studies director Tracey Patton remarked, "She's emblematic of what we all hope to accomplish in life. I think every person on this planet would like to affect positive change for the world. Very few of us get to do that but she did. She has made lives better in the state of Wyoming."

Political actors and community builders like Byrd help illustrate how issues of race and gender can be mitigated and how, once they are mitigated, effective political action can move a community forward. Byrd's love of community and love of place were steadfast and certainly provided a foundation as she encountered elements of racism. While these elements delivered a less-than-welcoming environment, Byrd remained unwaveringly loyal to her home state. As her early life portrays, the welcome mat is not always laid out for residents of the Great Plains. In fact, there is a great need for the vast and lightly populated Great Plains to better welcome all interested and potentially interested residents.

The fight to recognize Martin Luther King Day was perhaps Byrd's most visible contribution. In the executive order that established the day as a state holiday, Wyoming's governor tried to blend Wyoming political culture, the idea of an Equality State, with Byrd's broader vision:

WHEREAS, the year 1990, constitutes Wyoming's Centennial year of official statehood and should be recognized, respected, observed and celebrated by all people;

WHEREAS, the history of Wyoming has a unique foundation in diverse cultures, peace and equality. The name "Wyoming" was applied to the area by a newspaper publisher on his way to attend a peace conference in the territory. On December 10, 1869, the First Territorial Legislature granted equal rights to women, a "first" in the nation's history, earning for Wyoming the designation of the "Equality State." The State Seal carries the figure of a woman with a broken chain on her wrists, holding an "Equal Rights" Banner;

WHEREAS, the Centennial Celebration year of 1990 will be immeasurably enhanced by a holiday to properly observe, rejoice, and recommit ourselves to the principles of peace, social justice and equality;

WHEREAS, Dr. Martin Luther King, Jr. led a tremendous campaign that opened the hearts, minds and consciences of all Americans to the ideals of equality, justice and dignity for all people. Dr. King taught the importance of eliminating injustice through nonviolence, and has become a symbol for goodwill to all people. Dr. Martin Luther King, Jr. stood for, and articulated a dream and vision for the United States as represented in his words at the foot of the Lincoln Memorial: "Let freedom ring, for when we allow freedom to ring from every city and every hamlet, from every state and every city, we will be able to speed up that day when all of God's children black and white, Jew and Gentile, Protestant and Catholic, will be able to join hands and sing in the words of the old Negro spiritual, 'Free at last, free at last; great God almighty, we are free at last.'"

WHEREAS, In recognition of Dr. King's contributions, Congress approved and the President signed a law establishing a legal public holiday as the third Monday in January, dedicated to the birthday of Martin Luther King, Jr., 5 USC 6103. This day is unlike any holiday and should be separately respected as honoring the most fundamental details of the American dream, the American experience and our constitutional system. Its existence provides a vision, challenge and opportunity for all citizens to renew, embrace and live our nation's founding principles of nonviolence in the resolution of conflicts and the elimination of injustice; of goodwill to one another; and of respect for our shared values of dignity, equality and social justice for all people;

WHEREAS, W.S. 8–4-101(a)(xi) provides that the governor may declare any date appointed by the President as an occasion of national mourning, rejoicing, or observance of national emergency;

NOW THEREFORE, I, Mike Sullivan, Governor of the State of Wyoming, by virtue of the powers and authority vested in me by the Constitution and laws of the State of Wyoming do hereby order that January 15, 1990 shall be observed by State government as Martin Luther King Equality Day. All employees, not specifically required to work, shall be granted paid holiday leave from regularly scheduled work hours.

GIVEN under my State of Wyoming this 15th day of April, 1989.

Michael Sullivan, Gov.

As gracious as the order was, it only scratched the surface of Byrd's vision. It didn't truly capture the generosity of spirit. Byrd and her accomplishments were more accurately expressed in eulogies at her death. Senator Tony Ross, R-Cheyenne, said Byrd was "a lovely person and an advocate for people's rights," that she "left a legacy," and that "she was a person everybody loved." Senator Floyd Esquibel, D-Cheyenne, described Byrd as elegant, adding that her elegance was matched only by her passion for the causes she supported. "She had high principles and stood by what she believed," he said. Representative Mary Throne, D-Cheyenne, called Byrd a "legend" in the Wyoming Democratic Party and the legislature. "She remained true to her convictions," Throne said. "She's the reason we celebrate Martin Luther King Jr. Day in Wyoming. I think that's fair to say. She was always committed to the community, committed to what she believed and just a wonderful lady."

The Great Plains is not void of bad actors and actions. Leaders, and those who reside in the Great Plains or elsewhere, can benefit from revisiting the work of Byrd or any similarly oriented community leader. Their life stories provide a refresher course on how to engage in the deliberative nature of community and how to develop necessary virtues.

Conclusion

The six political leaders featured in this book embodied Great Plains virtues and values. They shared those attributes that identify the Great Plains as a region populated with community-minded residents.

They also shared this curious feature: all six made *food* a critical part of their work. And perhaps that is not coincidental for leaders living in the "food basket of the world." Wilma Mankiller wrote a cookbook, *The Chief Cooks*, and described how, in her cooking as well as in her role as chief, "I believe in blending and adapting to new ways while keeping the old ones always with us." For Mankiller, cooking was not only a useful metaphor but a source of wisdom for governing. Virginia Smith worked to find new markets abroad for Great Plains farm products, especially wheat, and she used her "coffee cake" communiqué to lobby her congressional colleagues. But she also felt a compelling need to address hunger at home, and she welcomed opportunities to partner with others to mitigate hunger through the Multiplication of Loaves Project. Junius Groves made himself into the Potato King, coming to own over five hundred acres in the fertile Kaw Valley of Kansas; he too was not satisfied with just personal success, and he gave away surplus from his crops to those who were hungry, asserting a powerful model for nearby farmers to be generous to those more in need than themselves.

George McGovern and Robert Dole worked together to feed hungry people. McGovern, growing up in a religious and caring family, observed families sharing food with others during hard times. He wanted to extend this sharing ethic to a national and world scale. He was a natural choice in 1961 as director of Food for Peace, and after his Senate career was over, it was equally logical for him to be appointed as U.S. ambassador to the UN Food and Agriculture Organization in 1998 and as the goodwill ambassador on world hunger in 2001. Similarly, Dole put food high on his list of political priorities, taking the lead in pressing for passage of the 1985 Farm Bill against Reagan administration opposition and working with McGovern to pass the 2002 Farm Bill, which utilized food gathered from the Great Plains to feed the world's neediest populations. McGovern and Dole were praised for putting their imprint on virtually every major U.S. program designed to feed hungry people—the Food Stamp Program, the National School Lunch Program, and the Special Supplemental Food Program for Women, Infants, and Children.

Elizabeth Byrd worked to feed the hungry in her own community. She partnered with the Salvation Army, the Federal Food Distribution Program, St. Mary's Catholic Church, the AME Methodist Church, and other groups to feed people without concern for their church affiliation, their party registration, or any other attribute except that they were hungry.

Perhaps it was a natural expression of regional interests for these six leaders from the world's largest food-exporting region to focus on feeding the hungry, but their concern also went much, much deeper. They recognized that food is a central part of community. There can be little community among people who are starving. But food is also one of the principal ways people express and renew their community bonds—whether in Fourth of July or Thanksgiving feasts, in community cookouts or church suppers, in potlucks for a school fundraiser, or just to socialize. Food, its preparation and consumption, *connects* people. All six of these leaders intrinsically understood the connections between food and building healthy communities.

These individuals are exceptional, but they are not alone in their commitment to community life on the Great Plains. A more comprehensive look at the accomplishments of civic-minded contributors to the region could stretch to fill an encyclopedia. Even then, the listing would remain incomplete because the stories keep unfolding. Many unheralded political happenings reinforce the notion that it is residents who weave the fabric that forms the Great Plains.

As we close, readers may no doubt be wondering, why *these six* instead of other notable Great Plains characters? This book could be recast in the framework of notable leaders, stewards of the land, or unassuming contributors. All such choices would be valid, but my framework offers a way to understand how persistent residents of the plains demonstrate a love and acknowledgment of people and place.

We all know of other, everyday heroes. For decades, I've had the good fortune of seeing immigrant students protected under the Deferred Action for Childhood Arrivals Program (Dreamers) enroll in my political science classes. Nebraska's Dream Act allowed Dreamers in-state tuition provided they had graduated from a Nebraska high school. These students imbued the classes with a sense of community; they were quick to acknowledge the help they received from family and interested community-minded residents. Their supporters had made sacrifices so they could find a better life in the Great Plains. The Dreamers fully illustrate the value of individual contributions to the greater community. Leaders know how to build from the positive contributions of immigrants and others who live in the Great Plains, from their love of people and of the land.

Some multigenerational forces aim to preserve the land for generations to come. For instance, a Canadian corporation's plan to transport crude oil from the oil sands of western Canada through the Great Plains states met stiff opposition in the region. Love of the land ultimately brought people together and reinforced their connection to each other and to the place; it created a deeper definition of community. Residents turned into activists through their public and political advocacy for protecting Nebraska's Sandhills from the proposed Keystone XL Pipeline. Pundits saw the dispute as a partisan battle, but that trivializes a politics more based on people's love of place. Jane Kleeb, a political activist involved in the opposition to the pipeline, aptly remarked of the plains culture in a 2014 *New York Times* article, "It didn't matter if it was 2 a.m. and driving snow, if your neighbor called to say they had a cow out or a fence down, you went to help." So when neighbors needed help in protecting the land from a destructive pipeline, the resulting collaboration and assistance were quite impressive. Ranchers, farmers, and local tribes—the "Cowboy and Indian Alliance"— joined forces to fight the construction of the pipeline.

Randy Thompson, a longtime rancher who opposed the Keystone XL, illustrated the stewardship called forth by the threat of the pipeline. He told Mark Hefflinger of Bold Nebraska, "I once said at a rally and now many of us remind folks often of this simple fact—there is no red or blue water, only clean or polluted. Ignore the color of your party on this one. Stand with our families."

Another threat appeared when the Nebraska Public Power District (NPPD), a mostly unaccountable public electric entity, proposed building a massive power-transmission line in central Nebraska. Named the R-Project, it would drive an approximately

8. *Leota watches a kite, Oyate Wahancanka Woecun Camp, Ideal, South Dakota, May 2014.* Photo by Kate Schneider. Used with permission.

225-mile-long high-tower line right through the mostly pristine heart of the Sandhills. Despite public opposition, N P P D persisted in gaining approvals for the project. One ranching family, Dan and Barbara Welch of Thomas County, sued N P P D in an effort to protect their ranchland in the state's most environmentally fragile region. Other concerned citizens mobilized as well. This example serves as a reminder that stewardship of the land and appreciation for the physical place is deeply rooted in the Great Plains.

Other examples of stewardship include the Native American protest against the Dakota Access Pipeline, an oil pipeline that was proposed to traverse the sacred land of the Standing Rock Sioux Tribe. Many concerned citizens joined the tribe in protesting this potentially harmful construction.

Pundits are far too eager to ascribe the political bantering around the Keystone X L Pipeline, Dakota Access Pipeline, and

9. *Branding day, Kilmurry ranch, Holt County, Nebraska, May 2013.*
Photo by Kate Schneider. Used with permission.

R-Project to partisan politics. Simple partisan explanations are often offered for the politics of the plains, but such explanations are inadequate to explain the cohesive nature of communities strengthened by those who love the land. As expansive as the horizon, a list of community-minded leaders would stretch across the entire Great Plains. Such leaders emerge for a variety of reasons, but a special catalytic force is ignited when the very land on which the community resides is threatened by less-than-appreciative human forces. Irish poets are inspired by the sod of their homeland, but Great Plains residents love their land as more than a temporary suitor. These cases illustrate the abundance of everyday leaders who hope to build and preserve the land for the next generation. Building community is enhanced by respect for the land.

Community-based respect for land is not always congruent with the beliefs held by those moving into the region, and it sometimes gets perverted into exclusion. In the spring of 2016, for instance, a Costco chicken-processing plant was proposed for Nickerson, Nebraska, a town of four hundred. More than one thousand jobs were to be created. Some residents opposed its construction because of the potentially harmful environmental impacts. Others did not want immigrants—documented or undocumented—to enter their community. Additionally, a few were opposed to the possibility of Muslims settling there, while others claimed their opposition was not about religion. Conversations about these issues cannot be ignored as we reflect upon the messages provided by this work.

The Costco chicken plant and the Dakota Access Pipeline may be harbingers of changes coming to the Great Plains. In 2017, political scientist James M. Scott surveyed current developments and found that "Great Plains economies are increasingly diverse, with strengths in agriculture, manufacturing, and energy, and exports are expanding more rapidly than the national rate. As the global has become local, the region has enjoyed growth and transformation." Such changes may stimulate deeper transformations in how residents view their communities and their futures, including their politics. One scholar, John Hibbing, in a 2016 issue of *Great Plains Research*, aptly observed that science might provide valuable insights into the political behavior of the Great Plains. Hibbing urged "students of the Great Plains" to continue to "[rely] on recent scientific discoveries for guidance in pondering the degree to which and the mechanisms by which the land and climate of a region can shape the traits and behaviors of the humans living on that land." Scientific study of the Great Plains does indeed give greater insight into the Great Plains political identity.

Those who appreciate the Great Plains as a special place know that "fly-over" country is worthy of more thoughtful and informed consideration. People of this area take pride in their virtues and style of living, characteristics that also infuse

10. *Human medicine wheel, Oceti Sakowin Camp, Cannon Ball, North Dakota, November 2016.* Photo by Kate Schneider. Used with permission.

their community politics. There are many more examples and people who could be used to demonstrate the significance and impact of Great Plains politics, but for me, the best examples can be traced to my mother.

My mother formed me into a student of the plains. I recall our rides from Bellevue, Nebraska, to my grandparents' house in Yankton, South Dakota. Being the youngest of nine, I was always either wedged between an older brother or sister or, better yet, I sat on my mother's lap. There were no car seats in the 1960s, but there was plenty of conversation. My dad was a son of Italian immigrants. Dad was fortunate to graduate from pharmacy and medical school at Creighton University; he was more fortunate to marry a beautiful blond-haired, blue-eyed recent nursing graduate—my mother. My dad's medical practice was immense, demanding his attention nearly 24/7. Our "vacations" were to Yankton or to weekend swim meets in Lincoln, Grand Island, or Hastings. My mom made these trips an adventure.

My mom's greatest success was teaching all of us—including my dad—the inherent beauty of the place and people of the plains. She would vividly portray what life was like on the Great Plains during the Great Depression as well as during prosperous times, when irrigation replaced dust and Mother Nature cooperated. Life in those small towns on the plains was focused on resiliency, and the people shared in successes and failures. In our partisan-charged political milieu, we lose sight of the reality that we can make a difference. Political scientists like to blabber about red states and blue states. Care for neighbors is not spoken of by the so-called experts. The lessons I learned from my mother were to be nice to everyone and that my happiness depends on me. My dad followed her "plains" advice and happily practiced medicine until he died at the age of eighty-five. I am still a student of the plains and still love learning more about it. Please feel free to join in my enthusiasm for the politics of the Great Plains and to build upon this short book with your own Great Plains knowledge and stories.

Thank you.

BIBLIOGRAPHY

Anders, Tisa M. "Groves, Junius George (1859–1925)." Blackpast.org.
    Accessed September 18, 2017. http://www.blackpast.org/aaw/groves
    -junius-george-1859-1925.

Associated Press. "Landowners Sue Utility Company over Transmis-
    sion Line Survey Work." 1011now.com. April 21, 2016. http://
    www.1011now.com/content/news/Landowners-sue-utility-over
    -transmission-line-survey-work-376572421.html.

Associated Press. "Smith Named 1998 Woman of Distinction." *Lincoln
    Journal Star*, March 7, 1998.

Associated Press. "Tiny Nebraska Town Says No to 1,100 New Jobs." Fox
    News.com. May 2, 2016. http://www.foxnews.com/us/2016/05
    /02/tiny-nebraska-town-says-no-to-1100-jobs-citing-way-life.html.

Associated Press. "Woman to Take Over as Chief of Cherokees." *Salina
    Journal*, November 18, 1985.

Avon South Dakota. "History of Avon." Accessed September 18, 2017.
    http://www.avonsd.com/editorial.asp?read-about=the-history-of
    -avon-south-dakota.

Biles, Jan. "A Town's Survival." *Topeka Capital-Journal*, July 16, 2006.

Biographical Directory of the United States Congress. "McGovern, George
    Stanley (1922–2012)." Accessed May 24, 2017. http://bioguide
    .congress.gov/scripts/biodisplay.pl?index=M000452.

Biography.com. "Bob Dole." Last modified September 9, 2016. https://
    www.biography.com/people/bob-dole-9276436#synopsis.

Blauwkamp, Joan, and Peter J. Longo. "Watering the Plains: Political
    Dynamics of River Preservation in Canada and the United States."
    Great Plains Research 12, no. 2 (2002): 352–68.

Brawley, Chris. "School Fights Tradition, Seeks Own Credibility." Newsok. com. March 2, 1986. http://newsok.com/school-fights-tradition -seeks-own-credibility/article/2139449.

Brown v. Board of Education of Topeka, 347 U.S. 483 (1954).

Brunkan, Melissa C. "Bob and the Bob-o-links: Singing to Brand the Candidate in the 1960 Congressional Campaign of Robert J. 'Bob' Dole." *Popular Music and Society* 37, no. 5 (2014): 557–82.

Byrd, Harriet Elizabeth. Family Papers. Collection No. 10443. American Heritage Center, University of Wyoming.

CCC Charter Act of 1948. Pub. L. 80-806.

Chalmers-Brooks, Katie. "Lifetime Achievement: Marion Meadmore." *University of Manitoba Alumni Magazine*, May 12, 2015, 16–17.

Cherokee.org. "About the Nation." Accessed September 17, 2017. http:// www.cherokee.org/About-The-Nation.

Cherokee Nation of Oklahoma v. Babbitt, 117 F.3d 1489 (1997).

Cherokee Nation of Oklahoma v. U.S., 124 F.3d 1413 (1997).

The Cherokee Word for Water. "Synopsis." Accessed September 17, 2017. http://www.cw4w.com/.

Chilton, James. "Legislature in Session on Martin Luther King Day." *Wyoming Tribune-Eagle*, January 20, 2015.

Chilton, James, and Becky Orr. "'Liz' Byrd, First Black Woman in Wyoming House, Dies at 88." *Wyoming Tribune-Eagle*, January 29, 2015.

Circle C Market. "Our Beginning." Accessed September 17, 2017. http:// www.circlecmarket.com/our-beginning.html.

City-data.com. "Bell, Oklahoma Profile." Accessed September 18, 2017. http://www.city-data.com/city/Bell-Oklahoma.html.

Cox, Beverly. "Sweet Memories: Our Longtime Food Photographer Remembered." Nativepeoples.com. November–December 2014. http://www.nativepeoples.com/Native-Peoples/November -December-2014/Sweet-Memories-Our-longtime-food-photographer -remembered/index.php?mid=1457&cparticle=2&siarticle=1.

Dakotas Annual Conference of the United Methodist Church. "McGovern: A Faithful Disciple." *Dakotas Conference News* (blog). October 23, 2012. https://www.dakotasumc.org/news/mcgovern-a-faithful -disciple/.

Dell, Pamela. *Wilma Mankiller: Chief of the Cherokee Nation*. Mankato MN: Capstone, 2005.

Dobrowski, J. L. "Student-Run Grocery Store Opens in Cody, Neb." *Tri State Livestock News*, June 8, 2013.

Dole Institute of Politics, University of Kansas. "Quotes." http://doleinstitute.org/about-%20bob-dole/quotes/.

Dole, Robert J., and Elizabeth Dole. Papers. Archives and Special Collections, University of Kansas. http://dolearchives.ku.edu/.

Donovan, Lauren. "'Dakota: A Spiritual Geography' Author Returns for Literary Project." *Bismarck Tribune*, June 22, 2014.

Drum, Peter. "Aristotle's Definition of Place and of Matter." *Open Journal of Philosophy* 1, no. 1 (2011): 35–36.

Edwards, Richard. *Natives of a Dry Place: Stories of Dakota before the Oil Boom*. Pierre: South Dakota State Historical Society Press, 2015.

———. "Oil, Culture, and What Small Towns Have to Teach Us." *Prairie Fire Newspaper*, September 2015.

Elbein, Saul. "Jane Kleeb vs. the Keystone Pipeline." *New York Times*, May 16, 2014.

Ellis, Jonathan. "FBI Mined Secrets from George McGovern's Past." *Argus Leader*, July 25, 2015.

Farm Service Agency. "Commodity Credit Corporation." Accessed September 18, 2017. https://www.fsa.usda.gov/about-fsa/structure-and-organization/commodity-credit-corporation/index.

Fenno, Richard F., Jr. *Home Style: House Members in Their Districts*. New York: Little, Brown, 1978.

Finkel, David. "Women on the Verge of a Power Breakthrough." *Washington Post*, May 10, 1992.

Fogarty, Mark. "The Growing Economic Might of Indian Country." *Indian Country Today*, March 15, 2013. https://indiancountrymedianetwork.com/news/business/the-growing-economic-might-of-indian-country/.

Frazier, Ian. *Great Plains*. London: Granta, 2006.

Fukushima, R. "Sober Truth: By Telling the Tragic Story of His Daughter's Alcoholism, George McGovern Hopes Others Might Learn from Her Death." *Saint Paul Pioneer Press*, June 23, 2009.

Hafen, P. Jane, and Diane Dufva Quantic, eds. *A Great Plains Reader*. Lincoln: University of Nebraska Press, 2003.

Haitch, Richard. "Follow Up on the News: Challenge Facing Cherokee Chief." *New York Times*, December 28, 1986.

Havemann, Judith. "2 in G O P Try to Block Pay Raise for Congress." *Washington Post*, January 7, 1987.

Hawkins, Autumn P. "Hoeing Their Own Row: Black Agriculture and the Agrarian Ideal in Kansas." *Kansas History* 22 (1999): 200–213.

Hefflinger, Mark. "Nebraska Rancher Randy Thompson's Open Letter to Senate on Keystone X L Vote." Bold Nebraska. April 30, 2014. http://boldnebraska.org/nebraska-rancher-randy-thompsons-open -letter-to-senate-on-keystone-xl-vote/.

Hendee, David. "From an Attic in Chappell: Ku Klux Klan Robes, Bits of Nebraska History, and a Mystery." *Omaha World-Herald*, May 16, 2016.

Hoedel, Cindy. "Volland Store Revival on Kansas Prairie Celebrates the Spirit of Founder Otto Kratzer." *Kansas City Star*, June 26, 2015.

Kansas Historical Society. "Exodusters." Kansapedia. June 2011. https:// www.kshs.org/kansapedia/exodusters/%2017162.

Kansas Historical Society. "Veryl Switzer." Kansapedia. March 2009. https://www.kshs.org/kansapedia/veryl-switzer/12219.

Klages, P. "Woman to Become Indian Chief." *Brisbane Courier-Mail* (Australia), November 19, 1985.

Klaske, Steve. "Bob Dole Drops by His Kansas Hometown." *Kansas City Star*, June 13, 2011.

Kristof, Nicholas D. "America's Failed Frontier." *New York Times*, September 3, 2002.

Leah, Richard. "Honoring the Legacy of Senators Bob Dole and George McGovern." World Food Program U S A. December 2, 2013. www .wfpusa.org.

Letky, Kelly. "Wilma Mankiller." *Mrs. Mediocrity* (blog). July 26, 2011. http://www.mrsmediocrity.com/2011/07/26/wilma-mankiller/.

Longo, Peter J., and Chrisitana E. Miewald. "Native Americans, the Courts, and Water Policy: Is Nothing Sacred?" *Great Plains Research* 2, no. 1 (February 1992): 51–66.

Mankiller, Wilma. Papers. University of Oklahoma Digital Library. https:// digital.libraries.ou.edu/cdm/landingpage/collection/WMankiller.

———. "Tribal Sovereignty Is a Sacred Trust: An Open Letter to the Conference." *American Indian Law Review* 23, no. 2 (1999): rev. 479, 480.

McDaniel, Rodger. "Very Little Equality in this State." *Wyoming Tribune-Eagle*, July 4, 2015.

McGovern, George. *Terry: My Daughter's Life-and-Death Struggle with Alcoholism*. New York: Plume, 1997.

———. *The Third Freedom: Ending Hunger in Our Time*. Lanham MD: Rowman and Littlefield, 2002.

———. *What It Means to Be a Democrat*. New York: Blue Rider Press, 2011.

McLaurin v. Oklahoma State Regents for Higher Education, 339 U.S. 637 (1950).

Moss, K. Marvin. "Votaw Colony Gives Modern-Day Insight." *Topeka Capital-Journal*, September 30, 2004.

Murphy, Matt. "Cheyenne Rep. James Byrd Seeks 5th Term in Wyoming House." *Wyoming Tribune-Eagle*, April 21, 206.

Newport, John Paul. "A Game Lives on in the Great Plains." *Wall Street Journal*, May 31, 2013.

"Nicodemus Flour Co-op." Kbfa.org. http://www.kbfa.org/wheat.html. (Site discontinued.)

Nicodemus Kansas. nicodemuskansas.org. (Site discontinued.) Oakes, John B. "Pork: U.S. Prime." *New York Times*, July 29, 1981.

Oppenheimer, Gerald M., and I. Daniel Benrubi. "McGovern's Senate Select Committee on Nutrition and Human Needs versus the Meat Industry on the Diet-Heart Question (1976–1977)." *American Journal of Public Health* 104, no. 1. (December 11, 2013): 59–69.

Overstreet, Glenda. "Close Look Broadens Horizons." *Topeka Capital-Journal*, November 11, 2005.

Park, R. E. "Negro Home Life and Standards of Living." *Annals of the American Academy of Political and Social Science* 49 (1913): 154.

PBS. "Sharing Stories: One Family's Story." *African American Lives 2*. PBS.org. Accessed May 22, 2017. http://www.pbs.org/wnet/aalives/stories/590.html.

———. "The Trail of Tears." *Africans in America*. PBS.org. Accessed September 18, 2017. http://www.pbs.org/wgbh/aia/part4/4h1567.html.

Pear, Robert. "Should U.S. Cut Funds for Child Nutrition?" *New York Times*, December 1, 1982.

Putnam, Robert D. *Bowling Alone: The Collapse and Revival of American Community*. New York: Simon and Schuster, 2007.

Raasch, Chuck. "The McGovern Few Knew." *USA Today*, 2012.

Roberts, Mary. "Thedford Unveils 'Lost Girls' Historical Marker." NBC Nebraska. May 1, 2016. http://www.knopnews2.com/content/news/Thedford-unveils-Lost-Girls-historical-marker-377748211.html.

Roberts, Steven V. "House Approves Funds on Fuel Aid and Jobless." *New York Times*, February 10, 1982.

Ross, Sandy. "The World Food Programme: A Case of Benign US Policy?" *Australian Journal of International Affairs* 61, no. 2 (May 22, 2017): 267–81.

Schwieder, Dorothy. "Historical Musings: Reflections on George McGovern, Teacher and Mentor." *South Dakota History* 44 (Summer 2014): 163–74.

Shama, Jake. "Bon Homme Zoning Board Approves Wind Farm." *Mitchell (SD) Daily Republic*, September 1, 2015. http://www .mitchellrepublic.com/news/3829659-bon-homme-zoning-board -approves-wind-farm.

Smith, Michael. "New Film 'Cherokee Word for Water' Shows Pivotal Moment in Tribe's History." *Tulsa World*, November 25, 2002.

Smith, Virginia. Archives. Love Library, University of Nebraska–Lincoln.

South Dakota Democratic Party. "Senator George McGovern Announces Food Drive Benefiting Feeding South Dakota." Press release. June 3, 2011. http://www.sddp.org/2011/06/senator-george-mcgovern -announces-food-drive-benefiting-feeding-south-dakota/.

State of Wyoming Executive Department. Executive Order No. 1989-3. "Martin Luther King Day."

St. John, Sarah. "40 Years Ago: 'Kaw Valley Potato King' Dies." *Lawrence Journal-World*, June 13, 2013.

Sturm, Circe Dawn. *Blood Politics: Race, Culture, and Identity in the Cherokee Nation of Oklahoma*. Berkeley: University of California Press, 2002.

Thompson, Jake. *Bob Dole: The Republicans' Man for All Seasons*. New York: Dutton, 1994.

Toppo, Greg. "Dole, McGovern Champion Free Breakfast." *USA Today*, May 31, 2006.

Trandahl, Nicholas. "Why Wyoming Has an Equality Day." *Weston County Gazette*, January 17, 2013.

Tupper, Seth. "McGovern Seeks Reversal of Afghanistan Policy." *Mitchell (SD) Daily Republic*, June 23, 2009.

United States v. Cherokee Nation of Oklahoma, 480 U.S. 700 (1987).

University of Michigan Library. "Wilma Mankiller." *Great Native American Chiefs: Wilma Mankiller*. Online exhibit. Accessed September 18, 2017. https://www.lib.umich.edu/online-exhibits/exhibits/show /great-native-american-chiefs/group-of-native-american-chief/chief --wilma-mankiller.

University of Wyoming. "UW Profiles: Harriet Elizabeth 'Liz' Byrd." Accessed May 24, 2017. http://www.uwyo.edu/profiles/extras/liz -byrd.html.

University without Walls Research Collaborative. "UWW Flaming Rain- bow." Accessed September 18, 2017. http://uwwhistory.org/uww -programs/uwwflaming-rainbow/.

U.S. Census. "Women in the Workforce, 2007." Accessed September 18, 2017. https://www.census.gov/newsroom/pdf/women_workforce _slides.pdf.

U.S. Congress. Niobrara Scenic River Designation Act of 1991. Pub. L. 102-50.

U.S. Congress. Senate. Judiciary. A1 Bill to Designate the Birthday of Martin Luther King, Junior, a Legal Public Holiday. 98th Cong., February 2, 1983.

USDA Foreign Agricultural Service. "McGovern-Dole Food for Educa- tion Program." Accessed May 24, 2017. https://www.fas.usda.gov /programs/mcgovern-dole-food-education-program.

U.S. House of Representatives. House Resolution 1237. 111th Cong., 2010.
———. Pub. L. 102-50. 102nd Cong., 1991.

Van Pelt, Lori. "Liz Byrd, First Black Woman in Wyoming's Legislature." Wyoming State Historical Society. Wyohistory.org. Accessed Sep- tember 17, 2018. https://www.wyohistory.org/encyclopedia/liz-byrd -first-black-woman-wyoming-legislature.

Verhovek, Sam Howe. "At Work With: Chief Wilma Mankiller; The Name's the Most and Least of Her." *New York Times*, November 4, 1993.

The Water Well. "The Bell Waterline Project." *The Water Well* (blog). January 28, 2014. http://www.thewaterwell.net/bell-waterline -project/#respond. (Site discontinued.)

Weinraub, Bernard. "President Signs Huge Farm Bill, but Reluctantly." *New York Times*, December 24, 1985.

Wheeler v. Swimmer, 835 F.2d 259 (1987).

Wichita Eagle and Beacon Publishing Editors. *Bob Dole: A Pictorial Biography of a Kansan*. Wichita KS: Wichita Eagle and Beacon Publishing, 1996.

White, K. C. "Population Change and Farm Dependence: Temporal and Spatial Variation in the U.S. Great Plains, 1900–2000." *Demography* 2 (2008): 363–86.

Wilson, George. "Funding for MX Survives on Tied Committee Vote." *Washington Post*, December 3, 1982.

———. "Lobbying to Save MX Intensified." *Washington Post*, December 2, 1982.

Wolters, Rachel. "As Migrants and as Immigrants: African Americans Search for Land and Liberty in the Great Plains, 1890–1912." *Great Plains Quarterly* 35, no. 4 (2015): 333–55.

Worster, D. *Under Western Skies*. New York: Oxford University Press, 1994.

INDEX